To the prominent maternal presence
in my life.

M.C. 1974

from BJD3

The New  in Profile

The New

MET in Profile

Stephen E. Rubin

Photographs by Alix Jeffry

MACMILLAN PUBLISHING CO., INC.

NEW YORK

To Seymour Peck

Chapter 5, "The National Institution: "Radio Opera,"
copyright © 1972 by the Ziff-Davis Publishing Company,
and Chapter 11, "The New Guard: Placido Domingo and
Sherrill Milnes," copyright © 1973, are reprinted by
permission of *Stereo Review*.

Copyright © 1974 by Stephen E. Rubin
Photographs copyright © 1974 by Alix Jeffry

Macmillan Publishing Co., Inc.
866 Third Avenue, New York, N. Y. 10022
Collier-Macmillan Canada Ltd.

Library of Congress Cataloging in Publication Data

Rubin, Stephen E
    The new Met in profile.

    1. New York (City). Metropolitan Opera.
I. Title.
ML1711.8.N3M595   782.1'09747'1   74-18007
ISBN 0-02-605800-6

First Printing 1974

Printed in the United States of America

Contents

Illustrations

Preface

This book doesn't pretend to be a study of the Metropolitan Opera company as much as a collection of profiles of its members. The subjects chosen give a fairly well-rounded sample of the Met's constituents. Some key personnel, I am sure, have been omitted, but that's what happens with all samplings. If there is a heavy emphasis on vocalists, it is because singers are the lifeblood of any opera house.

Some of the profiles are reprints. All have been updated and, in every case but one, altered in varying degrees. The exception is the Rafael Kubelik piece, written in 1971. In the interest of history, I have purposely left it as close to the original as possible. To me, it is telling that what Kubelik hoped to achieve and what he actually did achieve in his brief stay were light-years apart.

In the introductory essay, I have avoided a specific discussion of money because I believe that William H. Hadley, the Met's finance director whom I have interviewed at length in the following pages, does it far better than I ever could.

Finally, let me say that *The New Met in Profile* has no particular theme beyond what the reader himself can surmise from what individuals who speak in it have to say. The introduction, admittedly downbeat, is only one man's opinion. I hope he is wrong. But the opinions of others are found in the core of the book. That, in essence, sums up my feelings about the technique of writing interview pieces. An interview is about the interviewee not the interviewer. I believe that the writer who gets in the way may be very entertaining, or very literary, or very clever, but not a very good interviewer.

Stephen E. Rubin

New York City
May 1974

Introduction

T HE METROPOLITAN OPERA is trying to wend its way out of a horrific maze of multifaceted financial, artistic, administrative and labor difficulties. Such is the magnitude of its woes that the more vicious members of New York's music scene, joyful in their malice, are busy predicting the imminent fall of the house of opera. Their chatter is a negative, destructive and odious business. What is truly distressing, however, is that the more sober, realistic and knowledgeable souls are sometimes unhappily predicting the same strains of doom. Whatever the outcome will be in the Met's monumental striving to keep itself afloat, the early and mid-seventies will surely go down as an onerous era for the company, a period of continuous crises.

Lack of money, of course, is one of the organization's biggest headaches. Opera is an outlandishly expensive business, and the Met shells out about $24 million a year. But to blame all the company's ills on the almighty dollar is to avoid the issue. If the Met is on the brink of disaster, it is because of plenty of other equally important factors that are heavily stacking the cards against its survival. A house with all the money in the world would still be as shaky as a penniless organization, without the ·proper leadership—and that means men of artistic conscience who know what they are doing.

Finances aside, much has been said—and rather sentimentally
—about how wonderful the state of the Met would be had
Goeran Gentele not perished in that terrible automobile accident.
This is pure conjecture. The fact is that Gentele was not in power
long enough to reveal anything much beyond a winning nature
and an obvious and admirable set of good intentions.

Following his demise, and the understandable period of time
it took for the shock to wear off, the Met's board of directors
behaved poorly by committing the cardinal sin of wasting time.
The peculiarities of opera management today dictate that seasons
must be planned and cast *years* in advance. There is only a
limited number of genuinely first-rate singers, conductors, designers and directors, and the competition is fierce for their
services. In the United States alone there are an ever expanding
number of burgeoning opera companies—not to mention the
numerous existing houses overseas—and all of them want the
best. The price for time lost, therefore, is almost always paid a
few years hence in terms of the artists one has to settle for.

Either unable or unwilling to recognize this salient point, the
Met's board of directors forced Schuyler Chapin to sit with his
hands tied, for ten months, in the powerless position of acting
general manager. His post meant nothing; it was merely a stopgap measure to fill a void while the board tried to make up its
mind whether to trust Chapin enough to grant him—outright—
the job of general manager. When they finally got off their
asses, they gave him the job all right—but not like gentlemen.

Board president George Moore * immediately threw cold water
on the appointment by privately saying unkind things about
Chapin and by making public cracks such as "There wasn't anything better around the ball park. He was the best all-around
fella. Every decision involves compromises." This was a helluva
way to inspire public trust in the new head of the opera house.
Even after Chapin assumed his position, and had more than his
share of public and private imbroglios, Moore continued to berate
him. Late in 1973, those in musical circles joked heartily about
how much Moore and Chapin loathed one another. Ha.

Usually, almost any man new to a job like general manager

---

* Moore was replaced by William Rockefeller as president and chief executive
officer of the Met on May 16, 1974. At that time, the former president became
chairman of the board. What this reshuffling will mean has yet to be seen.

of the world's largest opera company is given the benefit of the doubt. Gentele became a hero before he did anything, and a saint of sorts after he died. Chapin, too, had his courtiers. The press, virtually smelling an underdog, hopped on the bandwagon and within no time made the general manager an instant celebrity. His notices read as if his wife and kids wrote them. For a brief moment, it was like Camelot. What seemed to earn him all this adoration were his forthrightness, honesty, apparent sense of fair play and warm and likable nature—a decided change from the coldness and efficiency of the Rudolf Bing years.

Like the press, the company itself fell behind its new boss— almost to a man—with blind devotion. Prior to the opening of the '73–74 season, morale at the Met had soared to a happy high. Singers, stagehands, orchestra personnel—everybody was in love with Schuyler Chapin.

All the goodwill notwithstanding, there is no way of getting around the fact that Chapin began his reign with a number of strikes against him. He had Moore's snideries and the board's halfhearted support with which to contend. But most important, thanks to all the publicity he received, it became common knowledge—with none other than Chapin himself as the major source of information—that the general manager had absolutely no operatic experience and would virtually have to learn on the job. And this is one job that does not afford time for the luxury of learning.

Unlike his predecessors Bing and Gentele, Chapin personally was not an unknown commodity in this country, having been in and out of the music business for years. A problem that arose from his being a familiar figure was that everyone knew he had never had a top post with its accompanying responsibilities. He himself spoke endlessly about being a "number-two man," and his facade reflected it. While charming, intelligent and socially adept, he radiated little authority or sense of leadership. He had won many friends, being a genuinely congenial fellow, but had not earned the professional trust and respect of a number of prominent people in the field. This was understandable, in a sense, because he had never really had the opportunity to dazzle with his professional achievements. Now that the opportunity to shine finally awaited him, there were those who feared that, at fifty, it was a little late for a number-two man to come in first.

That was the beginning. Chapin formally took over as general manager in May 1973. By November of the same year, the doomsday rumblings had already begun. To understand the myriad whys, one must return to the setup Chapin inherited from his short-lived predecessor.

As initially envisioned, the Met under Gentele was to be run by a lopsided troika. Heading the company was the general manager. Under him, with an almost equal amount of *artistic* responsibility and power, was the music director (Rafael Kubelik), the first in the Met's history. Under the music director, with much less power except when representing his superior, was the principal conductor (James Levine), also a first for the company. Assisting the holy trinity was a lesser trio: assistant general manager (Schuyler Chapin), artistic administrator (Charles Riecker) and technical administrator (Michael Bronson). On paper, it looked fine.

When Chapin moved up to the top post, the structure remained the same, except that his original position was not filled. This was perhaps unfortunate, but not earthshaking.

In dealing with any sort of team effort, the matter of chemistry must be taken into account. Will the team members balance one another, get on with one another, listen to one another? We will never know if the original trio would have worked. One must assume that Gentele knew what he was doing when he chose his artistic bedfellows. To question whether Chapin would have chosen the same mates is ridiculous. He never had the choice. It is now a matter of history, however, that the troika arrangement that he inherited did not work.

When one gets to the heart of the matter, it really doesn't matter what kind of setup one has at the Met (or any other opera house) as long as there is someone strong enough to call the shots by either leading a team to glory or by playing dictator. For the first decade of his twenty-two-year regime, Rudolf Bing, color him any kind of dictator you want, called the shots superbly. Later he floundered, but even then there was never any doubt who occupied the throne.

In order to exist, an opera house must have an artistic *raison d'être* and a leader strong enough to carry it out. Look at the houses around the United States. Despite a number of varied assistants and/or colleagues to aid them, Kurt Herbert Adler

(San Francisco), Carol Fox (Chicago), Julius Rudel (New York City Opera), Sarah Caldwell (Boston), Lawrence Kelly (Dallas), John Crosby (Santa Fe) are all the prime forces (in many cases the originators) behind their successful companies.

At the Met, it is not always clear who is the king of the jungle. Superficially, it appears that Chapin rules. But it is less a question of power, and more one of ideas. While he is not without some artistic vision, the general manager is an admitted neophyte when it comes to operatic matters.

It has been said of Chapin that he is the perfect front man to represent any organization. This is undeniably true. His strong points are mostly concerned with good form. A model gentleman, suave and smooth yet never supercilious, he could give lessons in the art of comportment. He'd probably make a superb protocol chief. This is not a put-down. Why not capitalize on a man's assets? The qualities that he possesses, particularly at the Met, should not be underestimated. One can go awfully far on charm. It also helps in the fund-raising department, in which Chapin is proving to be pretty impressive. And there is nothing wrong with having a popular general manager. It makes for spendid public relations.

But, if Chapin functions primarily as a front man or figure-head, this still leaves the artistic side if not unattended, then surely without the inspired leadership which can probably only be forthcoming from a musician. Someone has to pull the artistic strings and if the general manager is not the ideal man, the next logical choice would be the music director.

Within the Met's Gentele-conceived team setup, Rafael Kubelik's contract as music director gave him about 49½ percent of the artistic control. Time and again it was made clear by Chapin, and to a lesser degree by Kubelik, that artistic matters at the house fell under the province of the music director and his staff. It must be firmly underscored that these matters encompassed not only what happened musically onstage every night, but what happened from nine to five every day in the administration of the artistic realm. Without both these areas operating at an optimum, there can be no hope for high artistic achievements.

Since there is no reason to doubt to whom the responsibility belonged, the music director—to put it bluntly—bollixed things up. He was only formally in residence from the start of the '73–74 season, but enough could be seen before his resignation in February 1974 to predict that he would not work out.

Under Rudolf Bing, for better or for worse, the Metropolitan was a mostly glittering international museum, relying on the star system with a vengeance and being extremely conservative in terms of repertory and presentation. The accent, first and foremost, was on voices. The stars came and went, the casts changed constantly, the results were variable and sometimes smacked of "instant opera," but when it worked it worked gorgeously.

Kubelik envisioned transforming the Met so that the accent was no longer on voices per se, but where it belonged instead —on the music. To achieve this, he trimmed the number of operas presented annually, thereby allowing more rehearsal time for each opera, and assembled stable casts which, for the most part, remained an entity for the run of a particular work during the season. The reasoning was that, granted adequate rehearsals, the longer the same artists performed together, the more of a chance they would have to develop into an ensemble. And true ensemble singing and acting is what great opera is all about.

Being a seasoned conductor, Kubelik also valued the importance of a maestro to the success or failure of a performance. Even an average cast somehow works to greater advantage with an inspired leader. As early as 1971, following his appointment, Kubelik immediately called for an era of conductors at the Met. This was greeted with cheers because, for the past few decades, the pit has been one of the weakest cogs in the Metropolitan wheel. Beyond the employment of more talented maestri, Kubelik also aimed for a more adventurous and well-rounded repertory of operas.

Ideally, what the music director craved was beyond criticism. Unfortunately, what he said he wanted and what he actually delivered were two very different kettles of fish.

About a month before Kubelik resigned, there exploded into the newspapers what has come to be known as "the *Tristan* crisis," one of the nastiest and most embarrassing scandals to hit the Met in recent years. It came at a time when the going was rough at the house (both because of bad luck and ineptitude), and a scapegoat was desperately needed. The music director became the prime target.

A tremendous racket ensued over the fact that Kubelik was only in evidence at the house from mid-August to mid-November and then again from early February until the end of April. Otherwise, communication had to take place via the trans-atlantic telephone or the Telex system set up between the Met and the conductor's home in Lucerne.

This was a reasonable enough criticism, although when he signed his contract it was understood *exactly* how much of his time would be spent in the house. In other words, Kubelik was living up to what turned out to be a poorly thought-through arrangement. In any case, his being physically present so little of the time was only the tip of the iceberg, but a noticeable one, and it took another conductor to shine a spotlight on it. This was Erich Leinsdorf who, although perhaps unduly harsh in his very frank statements to the press, at least is to be congratulated for saying in public what many other people were whispering "*entre nous.*"

The *Tristan* mess came about as follows. For the first revival of its unanimously hailed 1971 production of the Wagner music-drama, the Met chose Catarina Ligendza and Jon Vickers to sing the title roles and Leinsdorf, maestro of the premiere performances, to conduct.

A Swedish soprano, Miss Ligendza is known in Europe as one of those operatic types given to canceling engagements, sometimes on short notice. She was the choice of Goeran Gentele who, it seemed, preferred her to the established Isolde of the day, Birgit Nilsson, and, when warned about Ligendza's reputation, was alleged to have said something to the effect of "Don't worry, I'll be there to handle her."

As a matter of standard procedure, the Met hired another soprano, Doris Jung, to cover the part of Isolde. When Miss Ligendza did in fact cancel, Miss Jung, who had never before sung the part, was generally felt to be unacceptable. Leinsdorf, who suggested that the Met find another Isolde, had actually warned them on earlier occasions that it was a mistake to have a standby who had never sung a particular part.

Isolde, like Salome and a few other odd parts, is extremely

difficult to cast in a house as large as the Met. If there are five sopranos of Met caliber in the world who can get through the treacherous role and be *heard* in the house, there are a lot. Schuyler Chapin, however, was able to locate one lady who, it was felt, might do the role justice, even though she had only sung it in small European houses. Her name is Klara Barlow, and she is from Brooklyn.

Miss Barlow arrived, sang the first rehearsal, and was greeted with the news that she had no Tristan. It seemed that Jon Vickers—another artist who, in polite society, might be called temperamental—had decided to drop out because—he insisted—of weariness. It was generally assumed, however, that Vickers left because of his dissatisfaction with Miss Barlow. To further complicate matters, Vickers told the press that the production was underrehearsed, an odd statement coming from a man who had arrived six days late for rehearsals.

At this point tempers were raging mightily and Leinsdorf—whose ire is not to be underestimated—livid because of what he considered the irresponsible way in which the Met management was handling the affair, resigned. Subsequently he relented, however, and the production's original Tristan, Jess Thomas, agreed to sing the first performance and everything calmed down.

Except that by then, most of the sordid details were known all over town. In a highly informative *New York Times* article which appeared before the January 11 premiere, Leinsdorf really let loose with a few punches. "It's the most amazing thing to me," he said, "that nobody ever says Mr. Kubelik thinks this or that. One deals only with Mr. Chapin. . . . They have these Commissars for Optimism sitting around there. There seems to be a conspicuous absence of the Metropolitan's much-touted musical direction."

Leinsdorf finally said it. In Kubelik's defense, he had been kept regularly informed throughout the whole mess. At one point, he had suggested substituting *Tosca* for *Tristan*, a move which was nixed by the general manager as being too expensive. But this was only discovered later. During the imbroglio itself, it was generally felt that the music director's absence was keenly resented.

It was surely a rotten stroke of luck that the incident occurred in the first place and that it happened while Kubelik was in Europe. But there is no way of knowing whether it would have resolved itself any differently with Kubelik in evidence. What is obvious, however, is the faulty planning that went into the casting of *Tristan*. Accepting Gentele's choice of Miss Ligendza, it seems that, considering everything, the Met would have covered itself better than with a soprano who had never before sung the role. This becomes all the more apparent when one realizes that the *Tristan* production was universally admired, and one would think that the Met would seek to protect it at all costs. Also, there is a psychological element. Comparisons may be odious, but there is no denying that Nilsson as Isolde is a tough act to follow, so why take chances? That the whole affair turned out "all right" was purely a matter of good luck. Had Miss Barlow laid an egg on opening night (as it is for the most part agreed that she did later on the broadcast), it would have been all over the Met's face.

As for Kubelik, there is far more to understanding his failure at the Met than merely explaining it away by saying "he wasn't there enough." It was bad enough indeed that he wasn't there, but that was only a fraction of the problem.

It must be reiterated again, and strongly, that on paper Kubelik's vision for the company was absolutely sound. He placed priorities where they belonged at all times—on the music. But it is one thing to think nice thoughts, quite something else to have the gumption, backbone and talent to bring them to fruition. All the goodwill in the world isn't worth a damn if it is mischanneled. One needs a certain kind of steel-trap mentality to tend to the responsibilities of conducting new productions and at the same time be able to cope with the nerve-racking, never-ending problems of musical administration at a house like the Met. Kubelik's past, both at the Chicago Symphony and at Covent Garden, seems to point to the fact that perhaps he is not really music director material, at least not for internationally oriented organizations.

From most reports at the Met, Kubelik was universally admired as a human being. But he was not greatly respected as a music director or, in some instances, as a conductor either. He was, so the people who have worked closely with him say, stubborn when he should have been strong, ignorant when he should have been wise, and generally temperamentally ill-suited for this most prominent and pivotal post.

Only a man of scope and far-reaching knowledge can possibly oversee musical matters at the Met. One has to have, literally at one's fingertips, an all-encompassing acquaintance with the international operatic scene. One also has to understand the American cultural scene, what will work here and what won't. Kubelik appeared to comprehend neither the former nor the latter, and in this he was what many feared—provincial. He might well be able to run a smallish opera company somewhere in Europe, but the Met, no.

Beyond these elements, there are other things that are either innate or never to be gleaned. For example, one either understands and has a feeling for voices, or one doesn't. Some of the greatest and most admired conductors have been jokingly referred to as being "deaf." This meant that, while splendid musicians and maestri, they simply couldn't hear voices with the sensitivity they exhibited in such matters as orchestral color, balances, etc.

Kubelik is acknowledged as more than a respectable symphonic conductor. But when it came to voices, he appeared to fall into the "deaf" category. At least in this failing, he has plenty of distinguished company. Witness some of the singers Toscanini favored and you'll hear a very mixed bag of vocal resources.

All of Kubelik's pros and cons result in the kind of musical leadership that was not so much irresponsible as wrong for the Metropolitan Opera. The largest opera company in the world, it must—if it wants to be the greatest opera company in the world—be run as an international house, not a provincial one. As such, it must employ only the finest talent available in the international marketplace.

It's a matter of concept. A level of presentation that might be acceptable, let's say, in Düsseldorf, just won't work at the Met. A perfect case in point—one among many—to illustrate an abysmal misunderstanding of what will go at the Met is what happened musically with the much anticipated new production of Rossini's wonderful comedy, *L'Italiana in Algeri*. Because of the peculiar setup of responsibility following Gentele's death, it is hard to say whether Kubelik alone is to blame for the mess, but it really doesn't matter. It is damning enough that, under his aegis, Kubelik allowed it to be heard publicly.

The production was built around the suitable and sizable talents of Marilyn Horne. She is a singer of such unusual and incredible technical accomplishment that to surround her with anything less than the best is simply an exercise in masochism for her colleagues. Tempting the fates, the Met went a step further. It not only supplied singers unable to cope with Rossini's florid writing, but planted a man in the pit whose understanding of Rossinian style was absolutely nil.

When the production first went into rehearsal, Miss Horne discovered to her utter amazement that Gabor Ötvös, a conductor of whom she had never heard (and who was allegedly referred to as a Rossini specialist by Kubelik), did not want her to sing the cabalettas which not only add immeasurably to the piece, but which she can plow through with the ease of a Maria Callas garnering newspaper headlines. Ötvös reportedly claimed that they were in bad taste, particularly within the framework of this "ensemble" production. Miss Horne soon made sure that her maestro ate his words, but the incident cast a pall over the proceedings and proved to be a telling preview of what was to come. That Ötvös didn't understand either the importance of the material or the luxury of having Miss Horne sing it is, in itself, pathetic. It only followed that his conducting and the casting of singers would reflect the same insensitivity.

There is no point in going through the other singers one by one. Some could never sing Rossini, and others could once, but not anymore. It was only Miss Horne, however, who met the music's rigorous demands. Not *one* of her colleagues even came close.

It goes without saying that it is extremely difficult to cast properly a work like *Italiana* today. There is probably no house that could come up with the perfect complement of singers. But almost any major house could have done better than the Met did. To start with, at least under the leadership of a knowledgeable maestro, the whole affair might have had a feeling for the idiom, for the wonderfully light, airy and comic style that makes the opera a masterpiece. But between Ötvös' heavy hand and a bunch of singers who sounded like they were either gargling or barking, the performances had nothing whatsoever to do with Rossini or valid music making in any reasonable sense.

One cites the *Italiana* fiasco because it is the most blatant case of starting off on the wrong foot, of totally misunderstanding both the music and the presentation of such music at the Met. There was no way for such a crew to avoid a shipwreck, but at least without the presence of a Horne it wouldn't have been so obvious. But once you've got a centerpiece like that, you'd better surround it properly or you're in for trouble.

And trouble is what the Met got. Harold Schonberg, writing in the *Times,* blasted the production with unusual vitriol and then followed up his review with a Sunday piece that made the original notice look mild. The latter was also one of the first in a long string of anti-Kubelik pieces. It should have come as no surprise; such insulting mediocrity presented at the Met would get under the skin of even the politest and most sympathetic critic.

Kubelik and Chapin also found other means to ruffle the critics' feathers. At the close of the '73–74 season, there were great uproars of complaint and disgust over the dreary level of general casting, both vocal and conductorial. The *Italiana* was but one individual production. This hue and cry referred to the norm. the *Times,* in fact, reported that it had received more anti-Met mail than any of its music staff members could recall.

This unfortunate state of affairs developed because of a number of factors, one of them seemingly noble. Both Kubelik and Chapin were determined to give Americans every opportunity possible to work at the Met. This is indeed fitting. Surely there should be no prejudice against Americans—as there had been in the past—and maybe the scales should be tipped a mite in their favor (of two equal artists, choose the local one). But that's it. Because when it comes to making artistic decisions, chauvinism should be the last priority on the list.

It is also touching that Kubelik and Chapin wanted to give singers nurtured at the Met (many of whom are Americans) a chance to show their stuff in major roles. This is a splendid idea if their talent is of Metropolitan caliber. Otherwise it is pure folly.

There is just *no way* to run the Met as a provincial, small-time operation. But that's what it began to look like during '73–74. Suddenly, subscription audiences were being forced to listen to singers, American or otherwise, who just weren't up to the assignments they were given. The casting smacked of laziness, of taking the easy way out, of lack of imagination, of a frightening lowering of standards.

No one is saying that, as an international house, the Met has to cater to a bunch of spoiled superstars. That is anachronistic thinking. It's still possible to call the shots and get the biggies. Any artist worth his or her high notes would rather work under stimulating musical conditions than under makeshift ones. Generally speaking, stars become stars in the first place because they are good. And if a company wants the best, it had better sign up the few real stars who are around. That many of them were born abroad doesn't mean a thing. Who's to say that the best is only available on our own hallowed turf?

Admittedly, it's duck soup for an opera company to say to a celestial being, give us a time period and we'll build our schedule around yours. The Met cannot always do this; a serious repertory house of its magnitude does not work that way. No one is denying that the Met has chosen a more noble but infinitely more difficult row to hoe in trying to impose stable casting. Simply from the point of view of logistics, it must be a nightmare trying to keep one cast intact for a run of an opera or specific time period. Multiply this by the number of operas presented annually, and one can begin to understand the headaches and heartaches involved.

The point is that under these self-imposed trying circumstances, the powers at the Met better know exactly what they are doing and be able to do it—fast. Time wasted, indecision reigning supreme, means that a desired artist is lost to the competition. Assuming an understanding of all of this, one would think that the Met would have doubled or tripled its artistic staff to guarantee that the switch from the Bing to the Gentele/Kubelik/Chapin system would be affected smoothly. But no, the Met is in a severe financial crisis, so the board, displaying a classic case of penny-wise and pound-foolish, decides to cut the artistic staff. And now that Chapin is minus a music director, he is probably operating the thinnest, most harried and hard-to-reach artistic staff of any major opera house in the world. Even Chapin, although a mite defensive, cannot deny that the Met is not only slow in casting, but behind most of its brethren.

Still, giving them every benefit of the doubt and particularly taking into consideration the understaffing and empty music director's office, it appears nonetheless that Chapin and his team can't seem to make up their respective minds or don't know what they are doing. Ask any manager of major artists what it is like dealing with the Metropolitan these days—simply in terms of finished contracts and specified time periods—and you'll get a kvetch monologue longer than any in Wagner.

One shudders to think of the fine artists the Met has lost purely because of indecision. There are a number of singers whose managers are pulling them out of the Met (partially or completely) because answers to questions are not forthcoming. And the managers needn't fret; in the cases of the really good artists, there aren't enough days in the year for the singers to satisfy all the clamoring bidders.

The results of the Met's current shilly-shallying and of the time wasted because of Gentele's death and the period of indecision that followed can be seen only too clearly in the unexciting casting that was the rule of thumb during '73–74, and in what is yet to come, particularly in the repertory operas, in '74–75 and beyond.

To make matters worse, with stable casting there is less chance of hearing second-rate singing only on occasional nights. Every opera house has its grim evenings—they're unavoidable. But when you're striving for uniform casting, and your initial cast stinks (witness *Italiana*), what one then gets is consistently unacceptable vocalism performance after performance.

Rather than single out individual performers, which would be unnecessarily cruel, it is just as telling to study total casts. Sometimes, miscast singers ruin an otherwise acceptable group, other times it seems as if the Met has lumped them all together —a stellar display of mediocrity running rampant. In any case, what follows are some of the less than glorious performances, listed in no particular order, which occurred during '73–74:

Carmen: Elias, McCracken/Lewis, Amara/Boky, Reardon— Lewis.

L'Elisir d'Amore: Peters, DiGiuseppe, Sereni—Rudolf.

Rigoletto: Quilico, Boky, Goeke—Baudo.

L'Italiana in Algeri: Horne, Weidinger, Love, Boucher, Corena, Alva, Uppman—Ötvös.

Il Barbiere di Siviglia: Goeke, Walker, Elias, Corena, Love, Tozzi—Pritchard.

It's hard to stomach, but there are enough performances involved here (and the list is generously conservative) to make up an entire season for a smallish opera company. How the Met can continue this kind of nonsense and, in the long run, stay in business is beyond comprehension.

It must be stressed that many of the singers listed above are not necessarily bad or ready for retirement. Some of them were simply miscast and could be singing other, no doubt smaller, parts quite honorably at the Met. All one is asking for is the right artist in the right role. And the right artist needn't be an international favorite or an American or a black or a Chinese, but simply a valid performer.

Why, for example, aren't some of the following singers and conductors at the Metropolitan? They are not all superstars, but they could admirably fill some of the house's more noticeable gaps. Where are Janet Baker, Helga Dernesch, Herbert von Karajan, Mirella Freni, Georg Solti, Colin Davis, Fiorenza Cossotto, Claudio Abbado, Renata Scotto, Zubin Mehta, Josephine Veasey, Seiji Ozawa, Pierre Boulez, Nicolai Ghiaurov, Margaret Price, Gundula Janowitz, Daniel Barenboim, René Kollo, Riccardo Muti, Elizabeth Harwood, Lorin Maazel, Ileana Cotrubas, Yvonne Minton, Dietrich Fischer-Dieskau, Teresa Berganza, Geraint Evans and Piero Cappuccilli? And, just for a bonus, where are Joan Sutherland and Luciano Pavarotti during '74–75? (Actually, both artists were more than willing to come to the Met, but couldn't reach an agreement because of repertory.)

No one is trying to ram these artists or any artists down the Met's throat. If the Met thinks it can present great opera in some other fashion, that's just fine. Only it has yet to prove it. Covent Garden, while enjoying a generous sprinkling of international artists, relies heavily upon its own home-grown cadre of fine singers, most of whom were nurtured right at the house. If the Met wants to build a nucleus of Americans or Abyssinians, lovely. But so far, most of what it is doing in terms of Americans is shamelessly raiding the New York City Opera of its talent.

Which brings up another problem. Is it fair to ask the public to plunk down twenty or twenty-five bucks to hear someone they can listen to next door for less than half the price? The answer is yes in the rare case of the greater artists because they are worth the price. But it is no in the case of the run-of-the-mill singers who are being used because the Met can't or won't find anybody else. Perhaps some of the latter personnel belongs at the Met, but surely not in important assignments.

Some of Gentele/Kubelik/Chapin's ideas have worked. By trimming the number of operas presented annually, there has been more rehearsal time. So despite some idiotic casting, a number of the war-horses have been presented minus that slap-dash quality that reeks of shoddy musical preparation. This is particularly true of the Italian repertory, which sometimes get such inhuman treatment one would think the Italian Anti-Defamation League would be on the Met's back. A lot of the credit here goes to principal conductor James Levine, who is slowly but surely cleaning up the mess in this repertory area left to him by the Molinari-Pradellis and Nino Verchis of this world.

But we have yet to see the promised era of conductors at the Met. There have been a lot of new faces in the pit, but none has made a startling impact so far. The orchestra, however, is for the most part, in much better shape, and is finally sounding like a major ensemble with reasonable consistency. So is the chorus, with a new man, David Stivender, finally in charge.

Kubelik's vision of a broadened repertory is slowly coming to fruition, too. It was surely about time that the Met gave New York *Les Troyens* (although it was by no means a total triumph, especially for its conductor, Mr. Kubelik). It was also a pleasure to hear *Italiana* (despite the aforementioned mishaps) and *I Vespri Siciliani* (despite a questionable Germanic production approach). And coming up are Britten's *Death in Venice*, *Jenufa* and *The Siege of Corinth*—all steps in the right direction.

In fact, it is a curious irony that even some of the Met's worst critics will admit that, here and there, some artistic areas are brightening up. If nothing else, it is pretty much unanimous among most onlookers that Chapin is trying. And these things do take time.

But while the current regime goes stumbling toward Nirvana, what is going to happen? What with its all-encompassing problems, particularly the economic ones, too long a period for the Met to find its identity will spell doom for the company.

And that's really what the mess at the Met is all about. Yes, they mean well. Yes, they have some interesting, even exalted ideas. Yes, some of these ideas have worked. But no, they are not working well enough or consistently enough. No, there is not an overriding artistic engineer at the Met, a man of true vision and backbone who can push, shove and force a dream to become a reality.

Rafael Kubelik called the music director the artistic conscience of a house. He was so right. And now that he is gone and his post is vacant, there is a most precarious void. Rumors have been rampant about his replacement, but it appears that, for the nonce, Chapin will go it alone. In any case, having been badly burned before, he will not jump ahead without giving the matter very careful consideration.

It is hoped that in the meantime, the general manager will take advantage of the presence of his principal conductor, Levine. Though he is admired as one of the most brilliant and serious of the younger maestri, Levine's post during the Kubelik period was never clearly defined. Nor was his expertise in operatic matters employed where it could have been. It has been said that Levine may, in essence, be the music director these days, but without the title. This may prove to be the perfect solution to a very sticky problem.

There are those who believe that the Met can only be run by one man. Others feel that a dual leadership on the order of Covent Garden's would be advisable. Still others claim that if a music director is appointed, he shouldn't be an international maestro with career aspirations because, no matter what, his major interest would be promoting himself and his productions. This group believes that a solid musician, perhaps an older man, who would be content dealing mostly with administrative matters and a light conducting schedule, would be suitable.

Of course, there have been a host of general managers who have operated successful houses without a music director. The Met itself never had one until Kubelik came along. But then the Met was never the kind of monster operation it is today. Can one man handle it all? Is Schuyler Chapin that man? With a strong music director, he might well make it. Without such aid, there are those who doubt his succeeding—primarily because of his lack of artistic experience.

The '72–73 and '73–74 seasons saw Chapin battle hideous luck in terms of the usual operatic cancellations and mishaps multiplied, it seemed, by the score. All this notwithstanding, however, he still made some ghastly errors in judgment. In his line of work, one has to think on one's feet and fast. Sometimes Chapin moved quickly but poorly, other times he was simply too slow. And a lot of his woes stemmed from bad planning in the first place.

Some fiascos, like the *Tristan* business, became public. Others were known only to the insiders. One night, the subscribers who came to hear *Vespri* got *Bohème* instead. They didn't like it. During the tour of 1974, Detroit got two *Don Giovannis* in a row. Was that better than what happened in Boston—an *Italiana* without its one saving grace, Marilyn Horne?

Hardly any of the people who arrived opening night to the new *Vespri* production realized that, morally, they should have been hearing Maralin Niska instead of Montserrat Caballé. Why? Because Schuyler Chapin, in a moment of very understandable hysteria and with the alleged full consent of his production staff, personally promised the opening to Miss Niska, who never asked for it, but was covering the part of Elena. He did this when Miss Caballé, displaying a cavalier and irresponsible attitude, kept on delaying her arrival for rehearsals. Finally, however, the general manager gave into a lot of pressure, and Miss Caballé, late though she was, went on. Does the inhuman emotional strain Miss Niska sustained get chalked up to "experience"? Or is it merely a dirty fact of operatic life?

How many other times did similar injustices occur? There probably isn't a singer alive who doesn't have a sad tale of mistreatment to tell, but that doesn't make it right. There must be a way of dealing with these impossible situations without sacrificing innocent bystanders.

One way surely is to avoid double standards. One cannot change the rules just to pamper a chosen few. If a house is not going to put up with star antics, that's it. But one can't accept guff from one artist and not from another. Because word gets around eventually, and soon nobody has respect for the boss. What a double standard does for morale is too obvious to be discussed.

One could cite other blunders as well as excuse them by

saying, "Give the man a chance, he'll learn by his mistakes."
Indeed, he may well learn. But again, *what happens in the
meantime?* Chapin and his staff are hard-working and well-
intentioned. But they may very well be gradually wrecking the
foundations of the company. It is no wonder that morale has
nose-dived. Sometimes you can feel *Götterdämmerung* coming.

An opera house the size of the Met cannot creak and grind.
It must run smoothly; it must have solid administration. It must
function between nine and five as well as between eight and
midnight. It is not exactly a secret that there were performances
during '73–74 that almost didn't take place. The Met cannot
leave itself open to any whims, be they of singers, conductors,
directors, designers. The Met can't be dependent on any single
artist to the point that that artist dictates whether the curtain
goes up or not. The Met must be prepared for any kind of
emergency, valid or otherwise. Chapin *has* always managed to
get by—but often by the skin of his teeth. Say what you want to
about Rudolf Bing. His house ticked like an intricate Swiss
watch. The current house clock is fast running down. Soon,
there'll be no time left.

1

The General Manager:

Schuyler Chapin

N FEBRUARY 12, 1974, Rafael Kubelik resigned as music
director of the Metropolitan Opera—a move that left
the company artistically in the lurch, but also paved the
way for general manager Schuyler Chapin to assume
total command, in actuality, for the first time. No longer
could anyone—including the general manager—proffer excuses
that he was either picking up the pieces of former administrations
or being cramped in his style by having to work closely with
colleagues, such as Kubelik, whom he did not appoint. Thus,
one could say that the Schuyler Chapin regime at the Metropolitan began in earnest on February 13, 1974. What happened from
that date on was his—and only his—responsibility.

Chapin's ascendancy to the throne occurred under the worst
possible conditions. Initially he came to the Met to assist general
manager Goeran Gentele. But when the Swede died a violent
death in an automobile accident in July 1972, Chapin was immediately hurled into the big time and named acting general
manager. Then a crisis of sorts arose involving confidence in
Chapin's leadership capabilities, which is why it took the board
of directors nearly ten months of shilly-shallying before deciding
in May 1973 to grant him the post of general manager outright
for three years.

A major stumbling block in Chapin's smooth succession was

that his operatic experience when taking over was virtually nil. Coupled with this weakness, he had never before been a chief executive. Feeling his way on alien turf, he also exuded no aura of authority whatsoever.

But once he became more familiar with the vipers' nest he had entered, Chapin's tentative stance altered. There was never really any time for him to learn on the job. In the notoriously shark-infested waters of opera management, one literally either sinks or swims. For a while there, it looked as if Chapin might sink. But no. Always extremely polished and charming, Chapin appears to have become tougher, too. In fact, the elegant and well-mannered New Yorker is proving to have more gumption than anyone—including Chapin himself, no doubt—ever dreamed him capable of.

Whether Chapin's more formidable and sometimes feisty new face is merely bravado remains to be seen—as do many other things. He has yet to answer one critic's gnawing question: "Can he lead instead of follow?" Now that he is on his own—there are no ghosts or scapegoats to shield him—the answer should soon be forthcoming.

When he first joined the company, Chapin was hailed far and wide as the original Mr. Nice Guy. Everybody, except for a few cynics who knew him when, liked the new man enormously and were willing to back him to the hilt. Then, with a fearful thrust in mid-1973, the Met's period of black adversity began (or at least became public), and it became instantly apparent that the house was in for a long, tough haul battling both financial and artistic problems. Morale, which had zoomed to a zenith, suddenly nose-dived. People even became fearful for their jobs. Chapin, however, remained in reasonably good standing, and still received the support of his company.

But the ebullience had waned, and the general manager's fans waxed less effusive. It is to Chapin's credit that he is no longer called Mr. Nice Guy all the time. Because you can't be a Good Joe and successfully run an operation as monstrously trouble-prone as the Metropolitan Opera.

All of this is not to say that one can ever envision Schuyler Chapin adopting the ogre's stance that seemed so congenial to Rudolf Bing's striving for a public image. Chapin lacks the salt of his predecessor and would not be comfortable in this guise. Nor could he excel in public duels with his celebrated employees as did Sir Rudolf with such splendid marksmanship.

Chapin is fond of saying that he shoots straight. "I'm a great believer, no matter how disagreeable a problem is, in laying the cards on the table—face up," the general manager says. "I am also not on an ego trip. Thanks to psychiatry, I do not feel the necessity to point a finger at me. I do, however, feel it necessary to be in charge and make decisions, which I'm perfectly willing to do, but not until I've picked the right brains. I *am* a brain-picker. I like to hear what people have to say. I much prefer listening to talking."

There are those who believe that Chapin has been listening to the wrong people. Despite his understandable naïveté and beginner's enthusiasm, he has already made some glaring *gaffes*. During 1972–73, there were an unheard of 170 cast changes because of illness and the general vagaries of operatic singers. In 1973–74, there were an enormous number of cast changes too, plus an assortment of major and minor scandals, many of which were played to the hilt in the newspapers and cast an ill light on the administrative and artistic abilities of Chapin and his staff.

These myriad incidents add up to monumental bad luck for Chapin, and though he rose from the flames, he did get badly burned. The general manager's casting policies—in regard to both singers and conductors—have come in for heated criticism.

One of the initial moves of the Chapin management has been to encourage the oft-forgotten homegrown talent nurtured at the Met. This means that if a singer covers a role and the scheduled artist falls ill, the covering artist will go on instead of a hastily flown-in replacement. It also means that the covers will get their own scheduled performances in major roles.

Not only is the company employing Americans within its ranks to greater purpose, it is also tapping that endless resource of native talent, the New York City Opera, and virtually stealing headliners like Beverly Sills, Maralin Niska, José Carreras and Harry Theyard, as well as lesser-known singers.

But it is one thing to support Americans, encourage unknowns and be generally adventuresome in casting; it is quite something else to foist a potpourri of aspiring singers on a subscription audience that is stuck with a scheduled cast. It is even worse to give that same audience a cast of has-been dullards.

Even before the '73–74 season had reared its sometimes ugly head, there were troubles in this area. On one less than memorable evening in the spring of 1973, a visitor to what is allegedly the world's greatest opera house could hear Marcia Baldwin and William Lewis in a poorly directed production of *Pique Dame* (*Queen of Spades*). Both Americans, Miss Baldwin and Mr. Lewis have been at the Met for more than a decade, appearing mostly in secondary roles.

"I have been criticized for the *Pique Dame*, which was an accident," Chapin says. "I have no defense. The choice of Marcia Baldwin is an example of somebody in a part totally wrong for her. It won't happen again. It's bad for her and bad for us. The problem that evening was, it was either Baldwin or a dark house.

"That is the danger of the kind of policy [of encouraging house singers] I'm talking about. On paper, I know what I'm trying to do is right. In actually carrying it out, it requires a much more careful selection of the people who are going to cover performances. If possible, I'm going to use these people nine times out of ten, and they'll work."

Chapin's sincerity in making such statements is not to be doubted. He not only means what he says; he truly believes in a number of the singers who both cover and are given scheduled performances. Unfortunately, the critics disagree with him, as do many of the subscribers and even some of his colleagues. The manager of an American opera company, commenting on what he felt were the shameful casting policies at the Met, remarked: "What astounds me is that Chapin has the nerve to advertise his folly by even casting the nationally broadcast Saturday matinees with a bunch of dogs. The *Barber of Seville* group on March 2, 1974, will surely go down in Met history as one of the all-time losers. Can you imagine putting Leo Goeke, Rosalind Elias, William Walker, Fernando Corena and Giorgio Tozzi into one cast? I wouldn't do it on a rainy Thursday night, and Chapin lets them go on the radio. It's incredible!"

There has been speculation that another motivation for the Chapin casting policy is an attempt to save money. However, this theory doesn't always fit the facts. Yes, house singers' fees are lower than those of the big names. But no, they are not lower than the cost of hiring an equally unknown artist and flying him in from Europe, just to get the imported product, the way Bing often did.

Chapin the idealist talks a good game, but he's not completely out of touch with reality. Had Joan Sutherland canceled a performance of *La Fille du Régiment,* by its very nature a star opera, he would have tried to replace the opera itself, instead of replacing her with a standby. Had this failed, "I would have gotten on the phone to Beverly Sills and said, 'I'm desperate.'" Had Miss Sills said no, "the cover [performer] would have gone on, and I would have walked on stage to announce it with armor plate."

There have been occasions when Chapin could well have employed an armored tank. As part of its legacy, the Bing regime left him a stable of singers who were past their prime many years ago, but were nonetheless retained and given choice assignments because they were favorites of the previous management. If these has-beens expected the same treatment chez Chapin, they were in for a rude surprise. "Some are going away very angry. Others will go away, I hope, by virtue of the fact that they've had their good days here."

One who wouldn't go away literally had to be bought off. She was once a leading Met soprano. "It was a very difficult thing to do," Chapin explains hesitatingly. "But it was impossible for her to continue. Every time she got on stage, she was unraveling her reputation. So we paid her what she was engaged for, and she left."

In another incident, Chapin ousted a conductor from a production as soon as it became apparent in the first stages of orchestra rehearsals that the chemistry between the music and the maestro was nil. In such cases, the general manager is in a pickle because, on such short notice, it is difficult to find a replacement. Chapin had to resort to a house associate conductor who, he claims, "did a very fine job."

Although he refuses to name names, Chapin has been known to be equally stern with some of the well-known troublemakers who think they can get away with being unprofessional because of their vocal art. Chapin is a great exponent of the star system, but in his mind temperament belongs onstage, not off.

"There are certain people who, by their very nature, are not content living reasonably smooth lives. A certain *agitato* element will always exist. I deal with these people candidly. I do not believe in displaying the trappings of power, but that doesn't mean I'm a pushover. You know, Peter Herman Adler once said to me after conducting a performance, 'I'll tell you something about this administration. It's very friendly, but very firm.' That's it really."

In 1966, when he was vice president in charge of programming for Lincoln Center, Schuyler Chapin collapsed on the street and had to be hospitalized because of a severe case of bleeding ulcers. He was furious with himself. "My father had terrible ulcers also, and died when he was forty-nine," Chapin recalls. "I was goddamned if I was going to go through this. Ulcers are emotionally brought on, and I did not want to spend the rest of my life clutching my stomach.

"So for three years I went through the terrible process of analysis. It saved my life. It was loathsome and awful, but it was during analysis that I began to think, 'Hey, wait a minute. Maybe I've been selling myself short. I've done a number of things, and they've been good.' That process was what made it possible for me to realize that I could do this job."

Since 1966, his ulcers have only bothered him seriously a few times—once, in particular, during the spring of 1973 when the Met's board of directors, undecided about giving him the general manager's job, gave him instead "a very hard time, which I personally never want to go through again."

Chapin's clothing and haircut, his general look, are extremely conservative—fifties Ivy League to a tee. Every so often he will jazz up a drab ensemble with a tie that is probably the wildest thing Brooks Brothers has ever carried. (His son Myles was amusingly taken to task by his father one Sunday evening at home for wearing a green tank shirt.)

His attractive and brightly colored office reflects its occupant. Chapin's large Itkin-style desk is the picture of organization, and it drives him crazy if he knows that folders are stacked there to be looked at. "Once," he says, "there was a week's worth of them, so I came in on Sunday at 11 and worked until 5. It was a heavenly feeling Monday morning when the desk was absolutely clear."

Chapin smokes eight to ten filter cigarettes a day, and never goes overboard "because the taste becomes terrible." He does not smoke until after lunch, nor does he drink during the day, "but take away my two vodka martinis before dinner and I'll kill you.

"Yes, I lead a very disciplined life. I like to be precise about appointments, and I'm trying to get people here to start a 10 o'clock meeting at 10 o'clock. When traveling, I'm dreadful. I have to be at the airport an hour and a half before the plane leaves. I need seven to eight hours' sleep, and I rarely go to post-performance parties. I'm in this theater at 9:30 A.M., and here almost every night. I want to be here. I'm not the world's greatest opera specialist, you know. I want to be in a position to talk with knowledge, not hearsay."

Most of Chapin's professional experience has been in the music business. Somehow opera got slighted, even though from age thirteen he regularly attended Met performances and developed into a rabid Wagnerite, frequently standing when tickets weren't available or when he couldn't afford them. Much of his youth, in fact, was spent daydreaming about becoming general manager of the Met.

He was not a happy child. "I guess I am a perfect example of someone brought up with an upper-class background—nurses, governesses and servants. I didn't even know my parents," he says rather sadly. "They used to come in and say good morning and good evening. We didn't meet very often."

His father, L. H. Paul Chapin, died when he was fifteen. His mother, Leila Howard Burden Chapin, was ten years younger than her husband. "A nice lady really, but we didn't have very much in common. I had two brothers, but we were not terribly close, either. There was nobody I could talk to. I was shy and had my own little world."

Apart from his fantasies, little Schuyler moved in chic, moneyed circles. His family goes back to the days when New York was New Amsterdam, and his distinguished forebears include the Revolutionary War general, Philip Schuyler. As a youngster, he knew the right people (John Lindsay, James Buckley), had the right relatives (Francis Biddle, Carter Burden) and went to the right schools (Allen Stevenson, Millbrook, Harvard, Longy School of Music). It was all wrong for him. By his own judgment a "very bad" student, he quit school before receiving a high-school diploma, much less a college degree (his stint at Harvard was as a special, unenrolled student), and went to work at NBC as a page boy for $15 a week.

During World War II, Chapin was a pilot in the China-Burma-India theater, flying more than two thousand hours. When he returned from duty, he went back to NBC, sold TV time, broadcast to the Arabs in English during the period before Voice of America took over the international shortwave departments of major networks, and was general manager of the Tex McCrary and Jinx Falkenburg radio and TV programs.

Chapin always seemed to know that show business was his métier; he also knew that, although music was his great love, there was no part for him on the creative end. This unhappy realization came rather startlingly when that grande dame of composition Nadia Boulanger, with whom he had studied at Longy in the hopes of becoming a composer, made her by-now historic statement to him: "My dear, you haven't any talent."

Not being able to write, compose or perform, Chapin headed for the business end. He was a tour manager for Jascha Heifetz and a booking director in the Middle West for Columbia Artists Management from 1953 to 1959. From Columbia Artists, Chapin went to Columbia Records (no relation) as supervisor of its Masterworks department. He then graduated to a vice presidency and was in charge of creative services. He lasted a year, then went to Lincoln Center.

At the culture complex, he organized the Lincoln Center Festivals of 1968 and 1969. During his Lincoln Center days, he came to know Goeran Gentele, then of the Stockholm Opera, and it was Chapin who initially pushed Gentele as a candidate to replace Rudolf Bing. In turn, Gentele persuaded him to come to the Met as his assistant manager.

Chapin's work history has been judged variously. A former Columbia Artists colleague was not overly impressed with the younger Chapin. "I remember him as a smooth talker, glib, suave and articulate. There was a slight *hauteur* about him, a feeling that all the work here was probably beneath him. Now he's much mellower. I guess I also feel he's a little bit over his head. There's nothing profound about him; he's a bit of a *schmoozer*. He's managed, nevertheless, to swim with the tide. He always lands on his feet smelling like roses. He has no great record of achievement. His is really a case of the Peter Principle come to sublime fruition."

Another music-business mogul says: "I have the feeling that Schuyler learns quickly enough to give a strong impression. At Columbia Records, Goddard Lieberson set the tone. Chapin carried out orders. But these days at the Met, he must be doing a lot of boning up. Recently, I heard him rattle on very impressively. Being so articulate and smooth, he wouldn't be embarrassed in any situation, I think, he's so socially graceful."

Composer William Schuman, who was president of Lincoln Center when Chapin worked there, reports: "I'm a great fan of Schuyler's. He's a man of perfect abilities. At that time, we were filled with ideals in terms of programming, and I needed a first lieutenant to organize the international festival. He traveled and lined up attractions, and I found him to be a first-class musical ambassador. He really cares about the performing arts as someone with much more than a layman's knowledge."

A manager who regularly imports attractions is not at all impressed with Chapin's Lincoln Center achievements. "People are booking things there all the time. I could bring La Scala in two minutes if I had the money to spend."

As composer Schuman says, Chapin is "to the manner born," a circumstance not to be underestimated in the rich and prominent world of operaphiles. Chapin's intimate acquaintance with the social set has been beneficial—except in the case of some board members "who've known me since I was in swaddling clothes and find it hard to take me seriously." Chapin insists, however, that there is an enormous difference between him and these well-financed folk.

"I am not a rich man," he says, designating his Met salary as being "not very large," and otherwise refusing to discuss it. "I've had to earn my living from the age of eighteen. I used to think, my God, I was brought up with the proverbial silver spoon. I was, but then my father died. Later, I was very fortunate because the lady I married, a fantastic dame, has a very interesting family herself—on the one hand, German-American; on the other, bounced-off-Plymouth-Rock Pilgrims."

The dame in question is the former Elizabeth Steinway, of the piano-manufacturing family. They have been married twenty-seven years and have four sons, Henry Burden, the twins Theodore Steinway and Samuel Garrison, and Myles Whitworth. Betty Chapin is, like her husband, outgoing and charming. For a woman of her social background, she is devoid of formality and appears to care little for outer trappings like clothes. No snob, she is the first to mention that the slipcovers in the enormous Chapin living room were bought at Macy's—on sale.

Mrs. Chapin might best be described by one of Mr. Chapin's favorite phrases—"right on." Hardly a member of the woman's movement, she envisions her role at the Met as being an important one, "particularly when nobody's seen a wife there for years and years. They've been wanting for a long time to use the general manager's box for friends of the opera. That's what we're doing now, and it's working out very well." On some Sunday evenings, the dining room table at the Chapin apartment is often scattered with lists while Betty Chapin busily juggles names to fill their box (six guests per performance). She obviously adores being the Met's First Lady.

With the Chapins' social connections, his two decades of experience in the music business and his innate gregariousness, the general manager knows virtually everybody in the New York arts scene. The fact that people almost always call him Schuyler has less to do with what has been dubbed his "shirt-sleeve informality" and more to do with his knowing them for so long. Chapin is particularly fond of musical show-biz types like Leonard Bernstein (a close friend and also a former boss; he was part of Bernstein's Amberson Productions before coming to the Met).

"I am a fan," Chapin says candidly, making no secret of his attraction to celebrities. "I have always enjoyed the company of talented people." Chapin's critics have gone further, calling him a hanger-on and claiming that his objectivity may become endangered when dealing with buddies like Bernstein, particularly when they become, in essence, employees of his at the Met.

"There may well be a conflict of interest at some point with Lennie. I hope not," Chapin says. "The biggest change for me in this job is that I cannot and must not get involved in the personal situation of anybody. It isn't a question of wanting to stand off . . . and yet I suppose it is.

"Everything is different now. I go to a cocktail or dinner party, and the thing I'm grateful for is that I'm over fifty years of age. So my name is in the papers, so people say, 'Ah, Mr. Chapin,' and turn around on the subway and buses. I'm a celebrity of a minor variety, which I find very amusing and take not at all seriously. I might, if left to my own devices. But fortunately I'm not. My wife—who thinks of herself as the world's biggest cynic, but isn't really—straightens me out."

Chapin isn't merely making conversation when he claims to be strongly influenced by his wife at home and by others at the office. According to Schuman, who has known him intimately for years, Chapin is a "virtuoso listener." These days he's all ears —and for good reason. The Metropolitan is snarled in deep trouble.

"There is no question in my mind that if we continue to operate the way we do now, in two or three years there won't be any more money," the general manager proclaims dramatically. "Unless the federal government steps up with money, I don't see where support for institutions like this is going to come from. We are seeing the end of the era of private philanthropy."

On March 2, 1974, Chapin greeted his radio audience with the heartening news that the National Endowment for the Arts was giving the Metropolitan a $1 million matching grant. This was coupled with an appeal for funds, and as of April 1974, the national listeners had sent in an impressive $550,000.

It costs the Met a fortune to operate, around $24 million a year. As Chapin himself says with utter amazement, "Do you know what we pay for the upkeep of this building alone? Two million bucks a year. Now, if nothing else, you'd think the City of New York would make a contribution toward that. If nothing else, you'd think they'd make a contribution toward the security made necessary by the conditions in the City of New York. That's $100,000 a year we pay to Lincoln Center. But take that goddamned $2 million—nobody sees anything of that onstage!"

What they will be seeing onstage will reflect, perhaps more than anything else, Schuyler Chapin's personal taste. The new production of *I Vespri Siciliani,* with its stark and symbolic moving platforms, is surely a hint of what is to come.

"In this age of over-image saturation and overcommunication,

I don't think it's right that so little has been left to our imaginations. It's absolutely ridiculous that in an opera production everything has to be forced down one's throat. I think that the combination of music, drama, color, light and dance is a potent enough basic series of ingredients so that you ought to be invited to find a visual complement to this. It seems to me that it's been like lining up the chocolate sundaes of the world and then throwing banana splits on top of them.

"I have rejected—and I understand that it may have been for the first time in a long time—a design for a work that is coming up. I rejected it because one does not need to build D. W. Griffith's *Intolerance* for a piece that is essentially a display work for soprano, mezzo, tenor and bass.

"There is a practical reason for this. We are sinking under the weight of the productions that we have here—the amount of stage labor that it takes to mount an evening, strike it, store it, etc. We cannot operate on the basis of nothing but massive productions just because it's a big stage. We really do not need *Lawrence of Arabia* and Cecil B. De Mille."

What Chapin is too polite to say is that the Met, at least under his reign, will never again allow the likes of a Franco Zeffirelli to spend a rumored million dollars to mount a shipwreck like *Antony and Cleopatra*.

Productions for the '73–74 season fell into the guidelines Chapin has set: *Les Troyens* ($400,000), *I Vespri Siciliani* ($250,000), *L'Italiana in Algeri* ($175,000), *Die Götterdämmerung* ($175,000), and *Les Contes d'Hoffmann* ($110,000).

As a further help in understanding Chapin's tastes in these matters, he lists some of the current Met products he likes: *Die Frau ohne Schatten, Fidelio, Der Rosenkavalier, Peter Grimes, Tristan und Isolde* and *Madama Butterfly*. On the negative side go *Macbeth* ("a disaster, even though we cleaned it up"), *Faust* ("I loathe it"), *La Bohème* and *La Forza del Destino*.

In the area of direction, Chapin hopes to bring in a lot of new blood and has already named John Dexter, whom he considers "one of the two or three greatest directors in the theater today," as production supervisor. He easily rattles off the kind of other talent he has in mind: Mike Nichols, George Balanchine, Jerome Robbins, Bob Fosse, A. J. Antoon, John Schlesinger, Peter Hall and Lindsay Anderson.

He's also eager to implement some Chapin innovations at the Met. For the problem of declining attendance, he has come up with a plan that is going to shock a lot of people. The 1973–74 season closed with 92 percent attendance. That may sound impressive, but each percentage point lost costs the organization $100,000.

"I want to make every ticket for every performance in New York something special," he says. "We play here thirty-six weeks, which is too much. To expand the spring tour is chancy and costs a lot of money. It's hard to get the big artists to tour because they don't like to travel. Therefore, ideally speaking, I'd like to leave New York around January 15 and come back at the end of February. We'd rent this theater in the meantime.

"We might go to Los Angeles, for instance, and stay there a month. The stars would gladly come. If they give us a month in New York, why not a month in Los Angeles? You cannot tell me that it is impossible for the Met to uproot for a month."

To assure further that the New York season is less taken for granted, Chapin devised a gimmick for the 1974 June Festival. For the first time there was a new production given during this period—the double bill of *Bluebeard's Castle* and *Gianni Schicchi*.

As part of the New York season, Chapin also wants to see a continuation of the Mini-Met "as a viable, small second company, but one that is part of the Met, not separate." The Mini-Met will be devoted to intimate and experimental operas unsuited to the larger hall, and will employ, for the most part, young singers. Marit Gentele, widow of the late general manager, is the executive producer of the Mini-Met as well as the popular Look-ins for young people which, Chapin hopes, will continue to be hosted by Danny Kaye.

Again in New York, Chapin is looking into the possibility of creating a Metropolitan Opera Sunday Evening series, presenting Met singers in programs devoted to unusual repertory, or at least repertory not currently at the house. These evenings would be in the guise of informal recitals with piano. Until this series becomes a reality, Chapin intends to rent the house on Sunday evenings.

Outside New York, Chapin is determined to take advantage of the fact that "the Met is this country's only national music institution. There is a history of seventy-one years of touring and forty-three years of broadcasts. In a proper way, we must cash in our national chips."

As for the broadcasts themselves, Chapin proudly announces that the Met has signed a new five-year contract with Texaco, sponsor of the program. He foresees no change in the format, which, he says, "has become beloved."

Television, of course, is the medium with the most potential. "Eventually," Chapin says, "TV in whatever form has got to play a role in producing income for this company. That means not only the initial broadcasts, but also the by-products. There's no reason why the Met can't produce programs *about* opera. I produced one (on *Fidelio*), and I'm not being immodest when I say it's the best film about an opera that I've ever seen.

"One has to turn loose one's mind. It's a matter of technique. Live performances from the stage have not, so far, been yawn-proof. We, however, tried an experiment with the first act of *Rigoletto*—with new equipment developed by ABC—and much to our surprise it turned out to be bloody good video.

"There's a big interest, thank God, on the part of the unions. They realize, too, that we've got to be in this field. This loosening up has made it possible for us to experiment. Eventually there will be regular broadcasts. The material, you know, can be cut and used in a variety of ways. The education market alone is enormous. The Look-ins could also be televised. I'm trying to develop a series of projects involving the Met in TV—and not necessarily with full-scale productions."

Another source of possible income for the Met is recordings. For the first time in fifteen years, a record company, Deutsche Grammophon, taped a Met production—*Carmen*. Chapin says he's eternally grateful to the German-based company, and realizes that future, expensive projects of this nature (the bill to Deutsche Grammophon was between $250,000 and $300,000) will depend in large measure on the success of the sales of the three-record *Carmen* set. According to a spokesman for the record firm, who refused to quote figures, "the album is selling much better than we ever expected, and has even placed very high on the classical record charts."

By an act of fate, Schuyler Chapin is the top banana at the Metropolitan—a novice with only on-the-job experience to guide him in pursuing what is considered the most harrowing and problematic post in all of the arts. A man with limited musical experience, he has lost his music director and will therefore have to shoulder perhaps more artistic burdens than he is capable of sustaining.

But music making is only one part of the Metropolitan. In order to be able to make music in the first place, the company needs money, audiences and a smoothly and efficiently run organization. Is Chapin powerful enough to provide all this, or at least powerful and smart enough to choose the right people to whom he can look for the right answers to help him make the right decisions? Is he a leader or is he a follower?

"I did not want this job unless I felt I could earn it," Chapin says. "I mean that in as simple and direct terms as possible. I cannot behave in a style that is not my own. I do not believe in making large pronunciamentos. I am simply not on an ego trip. I am going to do the work. We'll see what happens."

2

The Former Music Director:

Rafael Kubelik

WHILE HOVERING CASSANDRAS were predicting a bloodbath to accompany the succession of Goeran Gentele to the crown of Rudolf Bing, a scheme was already afoot to divest the new general manager of half his power. Author of the plan was Gentele himself, who recommended that the Metropolitan Opera be granted a music director—the first in the history of the company. To get the man he wanted, Gentele agreed to share equal artistic responsibility. Only under these terms, a virtual splitting of the kingdom, would Rafael Kubelik come to the Met. The contract was signed. Everybody was nonplussed, but when the shock wore off, jubilation set in, and the voices of doom were silent.

The new music director means business. The Czech-born Kubelik intends to transform the Met into a house where musical standards come before the varied whims of loud-voiced singers and money-minded boards of directors. "A general manager must run the administration for the artistic purpose which is set by the music director," Kubelik says. "Opera is music, and the music director is the conscience of a house."

To keep his conscience clear, Kubelik envisions inaugurating an era of conductors at the Metropolitan. "A conductor shouldn't be looked at solely as being responsible for what goes on in the pit," the sixty-year-old maestro says. "A conductor is responsible for the whole performance, starting with the production. I have always tried to influence the director to engage a designer who understands the musical colors of a piece. If these two or three people work closely together beforehand—and that means eighteen months with an opera—they can create an image which they believe the composer had.

"I think the whole stage business is overrated today. A director cannot go and stage an opera as if it were a drama. It's not a play. Opera has a special law, a special musical form. It's never as realistic as a stage play. It's not like a movie, either. Of course, one cannot have performers who are physically unsuitable for certain parts. One cannot have old-fashioned movements and all that nonsense, either. The director must try to keep things in good shape aesthetically and dramatically, but the main effort should be concentrated on the score. This means that the conductor is a constructive element in an opera house and that he must share the responsibility for the overall result.

"A conductor is not there to be a policeman pulling the orchestra into shape and giving the green or red light to the singers. Look, if a conductor doesn't trust his people, then what right does he have to stand there with a stick and say 'I conduct you'? Who is playing? *They* are, not the conductor. An orchestra and singers are a collective with individual hearts. The conductor is the soul and through him must flow the whole procedure from the first rehearsal to the last performance."

Kubelik's own conducting reflects this musical ideal. He is of the school of maestros which allows the composer to speak for himself. There is nothing souped-up or egocentric about his interpretations. They are tightly controlled, admirably disciplined and communicate only the music at hand. Kubelik's podium personality is far removed from that of the choreographic baton twirler, and only his Wagnerian six-foot four-inch frame and what's left of his unruly hair prove distracting on occasion.

Neither is Kubelik a headline maker. He talks freely and openly, on generalities rather than specifics. Individuals are rarely mentioned. Perhaps because he doesn't see himself as a superstar, he lacks the charismatic appeal of a Bernstein or Karajan. "I am not a vain man," he says. "I live for music, but I don't want to die for it."

Even before formally taking office in the 1973–74 season,

Kubelik began trying to engage the maestros who, he hopes, will guide the Met to musical glory. He has a plan for them. "I want to limit conductors and give them the responsibility for operas which they will stick to for years, changing only if they get fed up." This strategy should come as a salve to the countless Met critics who have complained bitterly about the absence of true leadership in the pit during the latter half of Bing's regime.

Those who have also denounced the stale repertory will exult in the knowledge that Kubelik is embarking on a campaign to freshen it up with works like *Les Troyens, L'Italiana in Algeri, Death in Venice, The Siege of Corinth,* and *Jenufa.* He also will cut the number of operas per year to assure more rehearsal time and a general uplifting of artistic standards.

Kubelik would also like to avoid the duplication of repertory that is currently going on full steam between the Met and the City Opera. "We should be colleagues," he says, "and work up a repertory that would be complementary. That two companies, which are next door to each other, play the same operas all the time is ridiculous. I tried to avoid this in London when I was music director of Covent Garden. I tried to sit down and discuss repertory with the Sadler's Wells. The first year we succeeded. And then . . . it is terribly difficult. This is the reason we would never do a *Makropoulos Affair* at the Met. It would be crazy. We shouldn't make our lives more difficult by being nasty to each other."

Kubelik has followed the City Opera's course closely and takes exception to the claim that it presents a great many rarities or forgotten works. "You know, this I must say: It was the same thing with Sadler's Wells. If they put on some opera of the same composer, like Britten, who was played in a big way at Covent Garden, then suddenly the press comes out and says this is marvelous. Because it's a small opera company and they want to help it psychologically. Certainly, the approach to these performances is more appreciative than if a big house does it. . . .

"I don't think the repertory of the Met is so terrible. A big house cannot afford to risk too much. I wonder whether it is just to say that the City Opera does avant-garde things and so-and-so and the Met doesn't. Look, I don't want to fight them, but their budget and their possibilities on a much smaller scale almost call for that 'little better.' They have the chance to try more because it doesn't cost so much money. The Met is the largest opera house in the world and cannot afford to be too audacious, but, of course, it should improve on its repertory."

In planning for the future, Kubelik will be able to fall back upon a sweeping musical training and practical experience of a diverse nature. Rather than being a specialist, the man is a consummate musician. He played the violin so well as a youngster in his native Bychory, near Prague, that his father, the noted fiddler Jan Kubelik, was sure his son would follow in his footsteps. As a pianist, Kubelik says he is an amateur, yet he was professional enough to play the keyboard for papa on a tour of the United States in 1935. Kubelik has been composing since he was seven, and continues to do so today when time allows. "I'm full of music," he says, "but sometimes I have to strangle my unborn children because I don't have time to put my thoughts on paper. If I could sit down right now, I could probably write you a fugue."

What has kept Kubelik from sitting down has been the lure of the podium and a host of administrative positions. As well as guest conducting the world over and recording prodigiously, Kubelik has held the post of music director of the Czech Philharmonic (1936–48), the Brno Opera (1939–41), the Chicago Symphony (1950–53), Covent Garden (1955–58) and, since 1961, Munich's Bayerischer Rundfunk, which he has built into one of Europe's great ensembles.

In 1942, Kubelik married the violinist Ludmila Bertlova, who had performed as his soloist with the Czech Philharmonic. Their son, Martin, who is currently studying architecture at Cambridge, was born in 1946. His wife died in 1961, and Kubelik was remarried in 1963 to the Australian soprano Elsie Morison, who had appeared in his production of *The Bartered Bride* at Covent Garden. Miss Morison has retired from the stage to be able to travel with her husband. Her swan song was as soloist on Kubelik's recording of the Mahler Fourth, part of the integral set of complete Mahler symphonies released by Deutsche Grammophon.

In his unassuming way, Kubelik has been consistent in following a life's standard he established for himself as a youth. When the Communists took over Czechoslovakia in 1948, Kubelik left and has never returned. Home is now Lucerne, Switzerland. "I try not to be sentimental," he says. "Of course, I was born near Prague, and all my life and music were Prague-bound, so to speak. But I feel that if I really want to live up to the simplicity of the Czech musician's approach to life, then I have to stay out. I cannot collaborate with people who are destroying the greatest wealth of the nation—the fight for freedom. Our nation was always bound to fight for its liberty in thinking and for its cultural treasures. This I can't do at home, but I can do it outside. So I must suppress my nostalgia. I always say that I left my country not to leave my nation. This is why I am sad, but not unhappy."

Kubelik found exile the proper solution to another of life's thornier problems. When he arrived in Chicago in 1950 to lead its orchestra, he came filled with the grandiose plans of a naïve thirty-six-year-old. Within a short time, because of his innovative approach, Kubelik was the center of a steaming controversy that split the city's musical community into violently disparate camps. After three years he resigned. "I never regretted Chicago," Kubelik says without the slightest trace of rancor. "It gave me a good lesson in how to look at the world from the other side. I came there like a fool, but I left in peace. My last concert was *Parsifal*. I did it on purpose, as an answer not only to the city, but to myself. You know, I performed sixty new pieces there in three years, forty of which were by Americans. And I don't count Stravinsky. One of the first was by a Negro. And, of course, I invited Negroes as soloists, which, in those days at Orchestra Hall, was almost revolutionary. I had my enemies. I had to fight with all those ladies. But I don't regret a minute of it."

This attitude typifies Kubelik. He is able to take things in stride. Even harsh criticism doesn't fluster him. "One is curious about the critics sometimes," he says, smiling. "A bad review is not very painful, but I don't deny that it is annoying. Particularly to read it the next day after you've given so much you are bleeding. In that sense it is painful. But there is something else. If, in a concert, I really feel satisfied with three or four bars, then I can call myself fortunate. There was never in my life an evening where I could have said, it really was as I thought it should be. And I have conducted thousands of performances. So why on earth should I be hurt by someone who feels the same way about it as I do?"

Kubelik's outlook takes on greater logic when viewed in the perspective of his *Weltanschauung*. "I'm much too devoted to life to be a fatalist. I believe in one's own destiny. I'm rather humble in taking things, but there is one great proviso. I don't regret anything in life, whether it was up or down. Because it all serves progress. One is always striving to improve. There is not one moment where I can say I did the right thing as I really wanted it. That doesn't exist. I always wanted more; I was never satisfied. On the other hand, because I was not satisfied, I was always happy. The search is the happiness. If I could say to myself today, I did things 100 percent right, that very moment I would jump out of a window because I wouldn't have anything to say anymore."

3

The Principal Conductor:

James Levine

IT TOOK THE Metropolitan Opera eighty-eight years to appoint a principal conductor to its staff. The first ever to hold the title is a short, plump thirty-year-old former child prodigy who garnishes his Humpty Dumpty-ish figure with bright red turtlenecks, zippy sport coats, patterned slacks and a mini-Afro haircut. The outer trappings tell only part of the story. James Levine is a live wire all right, but he is not a member of the wunderkind generation of overwrought and superficial podium playboys.

Levine is a jaunty, highly talkative and earnest young man determined to serve a profession he feels is currently being duped by fancy window dressing. His ambition is rather remarkable because he always knew where he was going and what the getting there would involve.

"I want to make myself obsolete in the concert itself," he says, relaxing in a cramped Central Park South hotel room. "I want to be able to have the conception seem to emanate from the orchestra members who are, after all, the ones with the instruments, instead of from the crazy magician with a stick who is making all the gestures and telling the audience what they ought to be feeling and hearing. I want to get to the point where the audience would have the feeling they didn't see me."

"I really think this could be done a good deal more methodically than it has been. I've had experiences with student orchestras that weren't technically up to professional ones, and that worked on a piece from scratch without any of the inhibitions the profession puts on you, and we got a performance that was unbelievably communicative. Something very much like this happened in a concert that the NBC Symphony played without Toscanini conducting. They did Dvořák's *New World,* and it was more intensely communicative than the one they recorded with the old man, though that one is neater."

Levine's confidence in himself stems from a lifetime's dedication to music. Born of a theatrically oriented family—his great-grandfather was a cantor, his father a violinist and band-leader, his mother an actress—Levine was already studying the piano at the age of four in his native Cincinnati. He made his professional debut at the keyboard six years later with the Cincinnati Symphony Orchestra. He then studied piano with Rudolf Serkin at the Marlboro Festival, and with Rosina Lhevinne at Juilliard and Aspen.

Despite an enormous pianistic talent, he soon found himself unalterably drawn toward the podium. "I never had a full-time piano career," the conductor says. "That seemed ridiculous to me. I practiced to be as good a pianist as possible, but I never really saw myself going around playing solo concerts on strange pianos all by myself in strange towns.

"I was a child prodigy talent. But I knew that didn't mean anything. I performed maybe two, three times a year, but there was no child prodigy career because my parents, who are terrific people, avoided it for me and I wanted them to."

In 1964, Levine (pronounce it to rhyme with *divine*) joined the Ford Foundation's American Conductors Project. On the jury at the finals of the competition was the late George Szell, who invited him to become a member of the conducting staff of the Cleveland Orchestra. He stayed in Cleveland for six years, first as an apprentice, then as assistant conductor, the youngest in the history of the orchestra, leading the ensemble annually as well as performing occasionally as a piano soloist.

Since leaving Cleveland, the young maestro has conducted almost every major American orchestra, and a number of the front-rank European ensembles. He is what is known in the

24

music business as a "repeater," being reengaged, often on the spot, almost everywhere he goes.

Levine came to the Met in June 1971 and made a highly successful debut conducting *Tosca*. During the 1973–74 season, once his appointment as principal conductor went into effect, Levine began spending seven months a year at the Met, and helping Rafael Kubelik supervise the musical aspects of the organization.

Levine explains his new position. "A music director has to see to the problems of orchestra and chorus personnel, rehearsals, assistant conductors who are assigned to musical preparation, casting, cancellations, understudies, all of this. Somebody needs to do this from the musical side of the general manager's office when Kubelik isn't there. That's my administrative job. I work with Kubelik when he's here and report to him when he isn't, because the final decisions are his. I do not want the responsibilities of having to act for the music director because I'm not the music director. Some day I hope to be the head of a symphony orchestra and/or an opera house. But I do not want the headaches of being a music director here without the rewards. Furthermore, I don't think it is fair for the major opera company in the United States to have someone making these decisions who is thirty. This is not true where my functioning as a conductor is concerned. Then I have as much control over the casting as is feasible."

The wide-eyed, bespectacled dynamo made his presence felt immediately at the Metropolitan. For example, in the '72–73 season, he was originally scheduled to conduct *The Barber of Seville, La Bohème* and *Faust,* but backed out of the latter two once he knew he was going to become principal conductor. He went to General Manager Goeran Gentele and said: "If I'm going to be a representative of the Metropolitan Opera, if suddenly I am going to appear to endorse what the Met does, then I have to be able to subscribe to my own performances.

"I don't like the *Faust* production—it's a disaster. I love *Faust,* I'm perfectly willing to conduct it, but I would give anything to be rid of having to conduct a production I can't stand. Gentele said, as it happens, *Otello* is open. So we changed to that. Later, I went to him on the same kind of issue for another reason. I had been assigned *Bohème* because Gentele wanted it revitalized. Then, I got a look at the casting which was done subsequently. Nothing wrong with any individual singers, but so many cast changes were impossible.

"Furthermore, that production is older than God, and while you might be able to revitalize *Bohème* with a new conductor and a stable, well-integrated cast, you sure in hell can't with a smorgasbord cast. *Rigoletto* was open; I looked at the casting and it was very stable. So I took it. This means that with *The Barber of Seville, Otello* and *Rigoletto,* I would have the kind of stable casting Kubelik and I were going to try to initiate in 1973–74."

Levine, whose repertory is probably as large as that of a conductor twice his age, is purposely concentrating on doing Italian operas. "I think this is where the Met's conducting staff has its real lacks," he explains. "There's a reason for it. Usually you'll get so many performances strung over a long period that no very busy, front-ranking conductor could give the Met that much time. For example, a set of *Bohèmes* will start in September and finish in February. Now, Abbado, Giulini and God-knows-who are not going to give the Met that much time. Therefore, when I begin to give them the bulk of my winter, it makes sense for me to take on some of these pieces. Hopefully, I can do something with them that will not have been done before."

Levine's energies are, at the moment, wholly consumed by his endeavor to become a greater conductor. He finds the time for the friends who will accept him on his terms, informally, and for serious relationships with women who are not marriage-oriented. In keeping with his open and outgoing personality, he is completely candid in handling these situations because there is no conflict within him concerning what comes first in his life—work or play.

"I've been really unhappy only a couple of times in my life," Levine says, "and the unhappiness was always musical. Some people think that the personal is the core and the music emanates from it. I think I'm an exception to that. It used to be that way for me, but it has changed. I tend to think of the individual part of me as being what I do musically. Therefore I place it as the most important thing.

"I have good friends who feel that their wives and children are the most important things in their lives. I find it difficult to achieve real empathy with that, though I understand it. My ability to function in involvements with other individuals has always been contingent on my feeling properly involved with music. When I am musically frustrated, unhappy, unproductive, my personal involvements are miserable. When my music-making is good, they are marvelous.

"The older I get, the less it seems to me that I could ever live my life with one person. I have had a relationship with the same girl for a long time, and I am convinced that our not getting married is very germane to it. I've been into all kinds of living, including communal ones, and I found them quite satisfying. Being able to relate to people freely without the legal structure produces various gradations in the way you feel about them and affects the kind of rapport you establish, which makes the 'one and only' concept kind of dim for me."

The basis for Levine's realizations were formed years ago when he was living with his parents. "One of the big fights of my life has been to make people understand that I don't have time for a lot of stuff they have time for. My parents could never understand why I couldn't sit for two hours lingering over dinner. It was difficult for them to realize that they had interrupted me from a problem that was on my mind all the way through dinner. From my point of view, if I solved the problem today, I could go on to another one tomorrow."

Levine illustrates his point by citing an incident which happened to him once and which he is determined will never happen again. "Years ago," he recalls, "I had a piano lesson in New York and didn't have time to learn the second movement of a Mozart sonata. On the plane I learned it, and played it by memory at the lesson. Now, I'm fast, but I refuse to perform under those conditions. I resent anyone who thinks that speed or flair or facility is getting into the music.

"I feel very keenly that I need the time to go over and over things, to restudy, to let them stew, to reach a point of view until I can go through a piece really certain, at this moment in my life, that what I'm doing is the best I can do, and that the best is good enough and something the composer would have accepted. I feel that unless one knows a score by memory, whether one is using the score or not for technical reasons, you don't have any right to step up in front of an orchestra and lead them conceptually.

"The problem is, everybody is looking for some kind of weird, commercial shortcut. Either they want to be, quote, original, or they want to capitalize on what somebody told them was their gimmick. I have a very low opinion of this, I'm afraid.

"Furthermore, I find myself totally disinterested in the question nowadays of technical proficiency, which literally seems to be the basis for evaluating an orchestra's performance up one side and down the other. You can read the words of composers from Bach to Stravinsky, and what you find them screaming into the night about is not the technical execution but the conception, the balance, the spirit, the purpose, what was supposed to be conveyed. To read Berlioz on this subject is so eye-opening you can't believe it. He performed in situations so primitive they would curl your hair today. We must now have fifteen to twenty orchestras in this country which Berlioz would have thought were a dream technically. But where is the piece? It gets lost.

"I have one real visionary dream, and I feel that everything I do draws me a little closer to it," Levine says excitedly. "Once in a while I hear a performance which is the kind of incredible thing that must have driven composers to keep on writing music despite unbelievable personal adversities. It seems to me there is a key to this which, so far, our system has not provided. I want to try and provide it."

NEXT FOUR YEARS
EXPENSES
20.9
19.7
18.3
17.4
16.9
15.0
14.0
13.8
13.4
OPERATING INCOME
'72

4

Money Troubles:
William H. Hadley

THE MAN IN CHARGE of money at the Metropolitan—no bowl of cherries these days—has a Doctor of Music degree hanging glamorously on the wall behind his desk, but it's as phony as Iago's good intentions. William H. Hadley doesn't know beans about music or opera. He knows a lot about business though, and has a businessman's way of cutting artistic pretensions down to size and getting to the crux of a situation. The crux of the situation at the Met is that it is in one of the worst financial crises in its history and, according to the finance director, "You can't spend more money than you've got, and survive.

"The fact that it's opera doesn't make it any different from any other business. And in any other business, if people cost too much, you use fewer of them. In this business, if you suggest a smaller orchestra or chorus, they say it's artistically not possible. I've never had the attitude that anything is impossible. Obviously you can get the chorus to sing louder, or something like that. You see, there's the nonartist in me coming out."

Before he joined the Met in 1966, Hadley, sixty-three, had seen two operas in his life. Since then he's viewed quite a number more, but exposure hasn't changed his perspective. He is still quintessentially a businessman. It is from this vantage point that he chronicles the background that led up to the Met's current financial jam.

"The most critical point in our finances is the fact that we've volunteered to say that the people who work here should have fifty-two weeks' guaranteed employment," Hadley explains. "It seemed like a good idea at the time. This way people like the choristers would have the chance to work full-time and not have to be shoe clerks for five months.

"We've built ourselves into paying for fifty-two weeks, but we can't put on fifty-two weeks of opera because we don't have the customers. I think that opera is just as seasonal as baseball. There's only a certain period during which people will go. For instance, we start too soon, we know that. In the middle of September, people aren't all back in the city yet, and haven't finished up their weekends. The tourists come to town, and if there's opera on, they'll go. But that isn't what supports it.

"Tickets have never paid the price in opera. Right now, adding up all our costs, we sell tickets for about two-thirds of what we should—which means that we'd have to charge about 50 percent more and chase away the audience. Historically, there's always been some kind of subsidy to make up the difference. In Europe, where opera really got started, the governments feel that it's their thing, and they support it. Our government has never really sponsored any sort of entertainment except Watergate. I can't imagine the senator from Kansas sending money to the Metropolitan Opera, which sounds like a rich man's place. He's got problems in Kansas he'd like to solve.

"What's been the subsidy in this country has been the contributions of people who wanted opera. The financial problems of the Met, I think, have always existed because we've been dependent upon these contributions to make up the difference between the price the public is willing to pay for a ticket and the price we've had to pay people to work at the Met."

If the Met actually presented opera based on the income it received from the box office, the final product would be far removed from what it is today. Specifically, there'd be fewer artists involved. Hadley explains why. "The expensive part is people— it's 80 percent people and 20 percent things." And it's not only the high-priced superstars (collecting as much as $4,000 plus per performance) who are breaking the bank. In fact, the financier claims that they are a small part of that 80 percent. It's the chorus, the orchestra, the ballet, the stagehands. Hadley cites the latter, for example, as costing as much as the top stars collectively.

"They really have a nice thing going," he says. "They start off with no training—except that they are members of families that have been in it, so they get in it. The average stagehand earns $20,000 to $25,000 a year. The orchestra members are geniuses, and they're getting the same amount of money.

"When you add up all the prices, plus the support of this building, which is $2 million a year, you get a people-oriented economic thing. And people are always wanting to be paid more because of inflation. Their being paid more creates the inflation. So you're starting off with a losing game. There's been no record of opera coming out even, except by contributions."

The contributors, alas, are feeling the pinch of today's shrinking dollar as much as the less moneyed folk. And therein lies the crux of the Met's current troubles. "The crisis today is very simple," Hadley explains. "It's been projected right along. If you have wage prices going up steadily, let's say 5 or 6 percent a year, and you have hit a maximum on ticket prices, then the amount of money you're getting for the ticket prices stands still, while the amount you're paying for people goes up. That gap gets bigger and bigger. Then, at a certain point, the people who send the money to make the difference say they can't send that much anymore, it's getting out of hand.

"The fact that it went from $1 million to $5 million in ten years hasn't been digested. If you continue that projection for another ten years, it goes from $5 million to $25 million. What you're really talking about is, first, the artists—orchestra, chorus, etc.—are getting paid more than they used to be because people didn't pay them very much, and, second, our dollar is shrinking. Inflation is nothing but a smaller piece of money. I bought my first car in 1938, secondhand for $350. A new one was $700. Right now, that same car is 7,000 bucks. That's less than forty years later and ten times inflation. The Met's gotten into this same inflation game, and we don't realize it. That's a big piece of this cost increase."

To lower it, the company has announced a number of drastic cutbacks, and there may be more to come. Most dramatic is the plan to work toward cutting annual employment contracts from a full fifty-two weeks to between forty and forty-four weeks, and reducing the current thirty-one-week season to thirty weeks (1974–75) and twenty-seven weeks (1975–76). Rumors are rampant that some future new productions may also be shelved.

Curiously, all the brouhaha over new productions is, in Hadley's opinion, a bit unrealistic. "New productions are critical from an artistic viewpoint, not a financial one," he says. "It's just like the book or newspaper business. You can't print the same stories all the time. I call this 'new ideas.' Whether they should cost as much as they do is another thing.

"But still, if you're spending $25 million a year, and about $1 million on new productions, that's 4 percent on new things. It isn't large, but it stands out because a new production costs between $200,000 and $300,000. My God, people say, how can you spend that much money when you say you're broke? So, in the 1972–73 season, we did only two, but our shop costs were still the same. We need to get a uniform volume, four or five new productions a year, and keep the shop running at a steady pace. People say, do it outside. But it should cost less here, provided it's cheaper in the first place—and not with five hundred costumes.

"Most of the foreigners who come over here, for example, think we're just going to open up the bank and hand it to them. The approach has been, this house is built for a lot of things. Well, it seems to me that the technique of the movies needs to be learned. You build a house that only looks like one, or you put something on a screen and flash it, instead of all this physical lugging around by our longshoremen. We're just like a cargo ship, moving stuff around all over the place.

"Our board is using a rather logical approach. They say, look, if we collect more money, it'll be spent. I agree with that. The habit here has been, the money's always shown up, so why worry about it. Now, everybody in the house is worrying, which may be a good thing. But it still doesn't help if there are too many trimmings."

Since, as Hadley explained, the Met refuses to use fewer artists, it instead is cutting the operating staff to within an inch of its life. Already, artists and managers are complaining bitterly that contracts are late and that answers to questions are not forthcoming. Hadley himself is rather horrified by the meagerness of the staff. "Christ," he explodes, "our artistic department is so thin, it isn't funny. You can't put on a show and keep track of all the detailed economics to see how you can do it cheaper with the same guy doing everything."

While by no means a voice of doom, the soft-spoken finance director is not optimistic about the future. He feels that shortening the season, for example, will only postpone future difficulties. He's also not sure that lessening the guaranteed employment period will be accepted by the unions. Labor, he claims, never goes backwards.

But there are concrete ways for the Met to earn more money. "Essentially, we've got to get a larger audience," Hadley says. "If you're going to say we have this many bodies to pay, and even if you cut some of the bodies back, eventually the price will catch up if inflation continues.

"Theoretically we keep saying that what supports such things as football are not the people who go to the game, but the people all over the country who watch it on television. We couldn't do that with opera—there aren't enough people who'd tune in—so we're looking into the technique of pay TV where you dial something and the price is put on your bill. That's one of the things for the future.

"There's also something else. I keep making this joke, but it really isn't one. If we toured all the time and rented the house, we'd be better off economically. We'd be getting rental income while getting tour income, and the tenant would be paying for the building. Another solution would be for the city to take over the building. But if that happened, we'd probably be so supervised we wouldn't know what hit us."

As for the much desired and sought-after support of the government, Hadley explains that it is neither forthcoming in any meaningful way, nor is it quite the panacea people make of it. Currently, for example, between what it gets from New York State and Washington, the Met receives about $2\frac{1}{2}$ percent of its annual expenses. This covers a bit more than a week's operation. And there are all sorts of strings attached.

"The federal government is absolutely committed to giving money only for new things, like the June Festival or the Mini-Met," Hadley says. "But they won't help you with the middle of the season where you're losing money. This is like commissioning an artist to paint another picture, rather than paying him for the ones he's already finished, but which haven't been sold."

There's another problem. All moneys from the National Endowment for the Arts are granted on a matching basis. "It was our hope that when the government said, match it, we'd go out and find new people instead of the same ones. But that hasn't happened yet," the finance director says. Usually, if the Met has matching troubles, it's the Guild, which is a separate corporation, that digs them out of the hole.

Last year, in a surprising move, the state government gave the opera house $275,000, about $150,000 of which was purely for its deficit. This, Hadley believes, was finally a step in the right direction, showing an understanding of the problems of any organization like the Met. And that is what it really needs money for—its operating expenses and its deficit, and not for new, perhaps more costly, projects.

"The New York State Council on the Arts has been very helpful and very reasonable," Hadley reports. "But they keep worrying that the accountants will come in and say, you gave the money for the wrong thing. Auditors are a group of people unto themselves. I invented a phrase a long time ago to fit their initials —C.P.A.—Constant Pains in the Ass. But, I suppose, if you're going to be an auditor, you have to be a sort of nasty old man."

No matter what, the Met is neither depending on the government nor asking too much of it. "If we could get on the order of $1 million or $1½ million, we could see the daylight," Hadley says simply. [In March 1974, the National Endowment came through with a landmark $1-million matching grant for the Met, not earmarked for any specific purposes. The largest grant of its kind to be given by the Endowment, the money will be used for operating expenses.]

While waiting for the dawn, the Met has taken to the radio, and on its first national broadcast of the season, December 8, 1973, Schuyler Chapin made a plea for funds to the wide listening audience. On future broadcasts, more of the same were repeated. The Met figures that about a quarter of a million dollars will be forthcoming from the listeners. Hadley believes that it may be higher. That, too, remains to be seen.

And so we come to the real toughie, the question that has been politely phrased, but is nonetheless ominous, and that is,

"What *is* the Met's ability to survive?" Can it? Will it? Hadley gets right to the point. "A shorter period without a fifty-two-week payment will postpone the Met's caving in, depending on how short a year we're able to work out. But it'll happen again unless we get a wider electronic audience paying more money. The whole entertainment business is in the same boat. We're selling 93 percent of the house. Nobody else is doing that.

"If we had 100 percent, we'd get even more money. But, if you fill the house for $50,000, and it costs you $75,000 or $80,000 to put on a performance, you see what happens. If you do three hundred performances, you lose $7,500,000.

"I have no way of predicting whether the Met will stay alive the way it's going. If people got out and worked their hearts out and came up with $100 million in endowment—which would feed us at least $5 million a year—then we'd have something to lean on, and if we weren't wasteful in the way we spend it, we could stay alive. Schools, the Metropolitan Museum stay alive because they have endowments. Schools without them close up right away. The Met currently has peanuts in its endowment, about $7 million."

It's not a pretty picture. And Hadley reports that morale at the Met, once at its zenith with the start of Schuyler Chapin's regime, is going downhill. People are worried, and understandably so. Suddenly they are being confronted with less employment, and always looming overhead is the threat, eventually, of no employment.

"Goeran Gentele always said, let's make opera fun," Hadley recalls. "We're shortening the season and squeezing it so tight that it isn't fun, it's a nightmare. We go through paper-clip saving programs and don't get at the guts of it."

As Hadley said before, "You can't spend more money than you've got and survive."

5

The National Institution:

Radio Opera

Opera fans are crazy people. They're really nuts.

"I'm not particularly fond of Milton Cross' voice," writes one listener to the Metropolitan Opera broadcasts, "but my dog loves it. As soon as I turn on the radio and Cross comes over the airwaves, the pooch remains glued to the set. When the music starts, he leaves. As soon as Cross is on again, the dog is back—all ears."

Opera fans are crazy people. They're really nuts.

"I don't know what is worn in an opera house today," says one elderly matron, "but on Saturdays I get my black velvet dress out of its box. And I dress my hair and put a fresh flower in a vase beside me. After all, I am to spend the afternoon with dukes and duchesses."

Opera fans are crazy people. They're really nuts.

Torn between his two passions—football and opera—one listener reports that when they're broadcast simultaneously, he solves his dilemma by means of an unusual compromise: he watches the TV set without sound while listening to the Met on the radio.

Opera fans are crazy people. They're really nuts.

A radio station in Norfolk, Virginia, ceased carrying the Met broadcasts when its manager found that he could no longer stomach the gripes of disgruntled listeners who jammed his switchboard on Saturday afternoons calling to complain about artistic and musical matters which were beyond his control—and interest.

TEXACO PRESENTS . . . the Metropolitan Opera. Welcome, opera lovers in the United States and Canada. This is Milton Cross inviting you . . ." The words are as familiar as the National Anthem or, at least, *The Battle Hymn of the Republic.* That's because the Met broadcasts are as American an institution as apple pie, hot dogs and baseball. Opera may not sit as well as any of those items among Americans as a whole, yet, for twenty afternoons every season, a devoted, hard-core audience of 1,600,000, as well as some 6,000,000 other occasional listeners, tunes in to hear "opera live from the stage of the Metropolitan Opera House at Lincoln Center for the Performing Arts in New York City."

Without its forty-two-year history of coast-to-coast broadcasts, the Met would be little more than a local phenomenon, a forbidding institution to those souls who had never ventured within its hallowed halls. Americans, unlike Italians and Germans, have no innate feeling for opera and its special peculiarities. Even today, the greater part of the American public looks upon this art form as a bizarre and unapproachable musical spectacle. And if that part is smaller than it might be, it is because, with a flip of the switch, the average guy, in the privacy of his home, can journey to the Big City and partake of what was once a pastime reserved for the privileged few.

While it is difficult to measure specifically what the broadcasts have done for Culture—even Musical Culture—as a whole, there is no doubt that, collectively as a nation, we have profited from the steady stream of Saturday afternoons filled with music. Others profit as well. Foremost, of course, is the Met itself. The broadcasts are good business; they have made the Met the national institution it is today. The company's annual tour may help, too, but the tour would be long forgotten were it not for the radio which drummed up business better than any public relations or advertising agency could possibly have envisioned. The broadcasts also assist the Met on its home ground. There may be box-office slumps, but they would be greater were it not for the out-oftowners who flock to see in person what they usually hear on radio.

The broadcasts have been sponsored, since 1940, by Texaco. What this "in excess of two million dollars" annual public service has done for the petroleum company is as difficult to calculate as what it has done for culture. But let Texaco try to pull out of its sponsorship, and the halo the company has been wearing for thirty-four years would become so thoroughly tarnished it would never return to its original glow. They've gained in prestige, that's for sure. No doubt the sponsorship has also paid off in dollars and cents. Texaco knows, via studies, that opera listeners are car owners. If they can believe the ten thousand letters of thanks they receive annually, there are a lot of people who appreciate them. These same people would surely rather drive a mile for Texaco than pull into a nearer competitor's place. Gas stations report regularly that customers are verbal and generous in praise of the sponsor. These laurels are garnered despite the fact that there are no direct commercials during the broadcasts. A four-hour opera, for example, carries only approximately one-and-a-half minutes of sponsor identification during the entire afternoon.

Record companies might also thank Texaco. Opera is the most expensive form of music to produce on disc, and, whatever sales are, they are boosted by the broadcasts, which whet the appetite for opera generally and for individual works and artists specifically. The record companies, while unable to cite figures, admit that when a broadcast of, say, *Otello* is scheduled, sales of that opera on records go up during the period before and after the air date. The companies further claim that the customer most affected by the broadcasts is part of the fringe public which doesn't usually buy the expensive multi-disc albums.

The broadcasts, then, are truly unique in a number of ways. Surely, they serve as an active catalyst to awaken interest in classical music and, by doing this, also stimulate various business enterprises. But most important is the unusually successful marriage between commerce and the arts which has worked beneficially for so many years. Of late, particularly on educational television, one can point to examples of large commercial concerns underwriting "high-class" cultural programming. But Texaco had the vision to be far ahead of its brethren. Today it can

claim the longest continuous coast-to-coast commercial sponsorship of the same program in radio history.

Before Texaco came into the picture in 1940, the broadcasts
were of a different nature. In 1931, the National Broadcasting
Company approached Giulio Gatti-Casazza, then general manager of the Met, with the proposal that they air a weekly series
of opera programs from the stage of the Met. Gatti was extremely
hesitant—fearful particularly that if the quality of the broadcasts
was inferior, the prestige of his company would suffer. But
business was bad, the money was tempting, and Gatti was
persuaded to hear a trial run, at the end of which the general
manager stroked his beard and declared, *"Benissimo!"*

And so, at two o'clock on Christmas Day, 1931, history was
made with a complete performance of *Hansel and Gretel*, broadcast direct from the stage of the old Met. The opera was chosen
because it took an hour, which was all the free time NBC had
at its disposal. Four persons—Milton Cross, Deems Taylor and
two engineers—ran the show, which was heard over the combined
Red and Blue networks of NBC—some 190 stations.

Throughout its first season, the program was only an hour
long, which meant, with most operas, that only excerpts could
be aired. In subsequent seasons, operas were presented in their
entirety, broadcast time being regulated by the length of the
works. When the Red and Blue networks split, the Blue, newly
called the American Broadcasting Company, took over the show.
It was a success beyond everyone's expectations, and it lasted on
ABC from 1946 to 1958, when CBS took over.

During the first nine seasons, the operas were sponsored at
various times by the American Tobacco Company, Lambert
Pharmaceuticals and the Radio Corporation of America. For
most of this period, however, the Met broadcasts were an NBC
sustaining program.

In 1960, another historic move was made. Texaco hired G. H.
Johnston, who still packages the show for them, and he created
and developed the now famed Texaco–Metropolitan Opera Radio
Network. This was done for a number of reasons, all of them
practical. By 1960, the Met had been in association with all three
prime networks, none of which was able to overcome some
hazardous inherent problems.

The major offender was "DB"—delayed broadcasting. If something more interesting or, in their opinion, more important came up, individual stations would broadcast the operas at whatever time they felt it most convenient—nine o'clock Saturday morning, midnight on Sunday or whenever. This brought in a plethora of complaining letters from disoriented and unhappy opera lovers. "Opera fans are crazy people," Gerry Johnston says with a knowing smile. "They're really nuts. They want the broadcasts live. Presumably it's because the fans can tell if the singers are hitting the right notes or not. They realize that on tape the note can be changed." (This happened only once in the history of the broadcasts when, in the Mad Scene from *Lucia di Lammermoor,* Lily Pons missed an E-flat which was later dubbed in.)

And so the Texaco–Metropolitan Network was born. Today it comprises 145 commercial stations and about 100 college (noncommercial) stations. Setting up a new network was more expensive than buying time on an existing one, but at least Johnston could make the stations "sign in blood" to observe the following rules: the operas must be carried for the whole twenty-week season; they must be carried in their entirety; they must be carried live. The only delayed broadcasting is to Alaska, Hawaii and Puerto Rico, which get the program the following week. The Voice of America is also given a tape of the broadcasts.

There are instances in which the rules can be broken, but only as follows: if, for example, a station feels the need to carry a local news event at the time of the opera broadcast it may do so—but not before it has found a competitor willing to take over its obligation and to advertise that it is going to do so at least two weeks before air date.

Johnston is a tough man to deal with when it comes to breaking the ground rules, but, he claims, he never forces stations to join the network in the first place, and when they do they must stick to the agreement. The college stations are all unsolicited. Whether consciously or not, Johnston's mania for consistency in broadcasting schedules has, in one sense, dictated the program's success. There is nothing easier to get used to than a program that is on every Saturday for twenty or twenty-one weeks—same time, same station. Many cultural experts believe that if television would try scheduling serious music on a more regular basis, it would have greater success with it than it has had in the past.

Television might also look to the setup of the broadcasts as a model of how to get along with the various powers that be. The Met itself does little more than offer its facilities, schedule operas and assign casts. G. H. Johnston is responsible for the actual technical pickup of the stage presentation. (Fourteen stage mikes, hidden in strategic locations, follow the action. For obvious reasons, singers are never told which mikes are on or where they are to be found.) Texaco pays the bills. The lines are clearly drawn, and the bounds are never overstepped. Texaco, for example, cannot and does not dictate to the Met about artistic matters. "The secret of our success is that we don't run into so-called 'policy differences,'" an official of the petroleum company explains. The Met, in turn, cannot tell Johnston how to run his network, and Johnston, who couldn't care less about opera himself, wouldn't think of asking the Met to schedule *Die Walküre* instead of *Sonnambula* or Birgit Nilsson instead of Joan Sutherland.

Which brings us to the intermission and the entry of another power—one to reckon with. Geraldine Souvaine, producer of the intermission features, has been associated with the talk part of the music program ever since Texaco took over in 1940. A thrice-married widow, she is knowledgeable, driven and tough. "My life is run by ideas, personalities and a stopwatch," she says, complaining. "It's awful." Miss Souvaine, or Geri, as she's known in the music world, proudly announces: "There's an unwritten law. Texaco doesn't interfere with repertoire and casting, and the Met doesn't interfere with my intermission features."

No one at the Met will say so for the record, but Miss Souvaine is not exactly a favorite at the house. She herself admits, rather extravagantly, "I'm at the top of their bitch list." The reason for the tension and clashing of wills is simple. Politically —and the opera world is wildly political—the intermission features are as prestigious and valuable as the broadcasts themselves. If the Met controlled them, all sorts of things could be accomplished. But with as strong-minded a lady as Miss Souvaine running the show, their hands are tied.

The Metropolitan's former general manager, Rudolf Bing, tried to force the producer to have certain artists on her shows, but to no avail. "*Most* artists want to get on," she explains, "but they have first to be articulate, opinionated and intelligent. Out of one hundred on the roster, I don't think there are twenty-five who are any good. My favorites are Birgit Nilsson, Ezio Flagello, William Walker, Martina Arroyo, Marilyn Horne, James Mc-Cracken, John Alexander and Joan Sutherland. We once had a singers' roundtable with Arroyo, Horne and Sutherland, and I got letters all summer long."

Miss Souvaine, who works with an assistant and two secretaries, is solely responsible for all the spoken dialogue of the broadcast that does not emanate from the Met's stage. This includes announcer Milton Cross' script, plus the various features which are inserted during intermissions, the number depending on how many acts an opera has. "I have to keep people listening," Miss Souvaine says simply. "The first intermission should have some intrigue. And it should be interesting to people without talking up or talking down."

Boris Goldovsky is frequently her choice to contribute some intrigue to these shows. He is usually involved in explaining musical matters. Miss Souvaine proudly recalls his talk on *Pelléas et Mélisande,* which prompted a letter from one grateful listener who said that even though he had never enjoyed or understood the opera, thanks to Goldovsky, he would listen to it anyway, realizing nonetheless that he still wouldn't like it.

The second intermission, and the most popular one, is the Opera Quiz. The third is Biographies in Music, with the Met's Assistant Manager, Francis Robinson, as host. To keep the features fresh, Miss Souvaine tries out various innovations from time to time, such as a singers' roundtable, a musicians' roundtable or a quiz with panelists taken from the ranks of the Met's ushers.

Despite her many other problems, Miss Souvaine can rest easy in the knowledge that she has on her side, in announcer Milton Cross, the man most identified with opera in this country. Dubbed "The Voice of the Met," or "Mr. Opera," Cross, who prefers not to have his age mentioned (he is beyond the seventy mark), has been associated with the broadcasts since their beginnings in 1931. In all—never missing a show—he has told the story of the opera being broadcast at more than eight hundred performances.

A student of singing, composition, and theory, Cross, a New Yorker, first came to radio in 1922 at station WJZ in Newark, New Jersey. His first job, short-lived, was singing ballads. His second was as an announcer, and he did everything from reporting on Herbert Hoover's inauguration to reading children's stories. He later got the Met job, he explains, "because I was the only one around there who knew anything about classical music."

Until 1940 and the arrival of producer Souvaine, Cross himself was responsible for all his spoken material. Today he receives a script two days in advance of the broadcast, and, for the small number of off-the-cuff remarks he has to make, he comes prepared with ad-lib notes.

Should there be emergencies, Cross has the experience of a veteran trouper to back him up. His record for ad-libs took place before the Met broadcasts began, when he was announcing for the Chicago Civic Opera. He had to talk nonstop for half an hour while the company's director read his annual fiscal report to the audience. Cross did everything from telling the plot of *Il Trovatore* (which takes some doing) to describing dressing rooms and the number of pieces of scenery and trunks needed for the opera's forthcoming tour. His success was such that he was commended on the editorial page of the *New York Herald Tribune.*

Perhaps the greatest crisis in the history of the broadcasts occurred on February 2, 1963. The opera scheduled for the day was *Der Fliegende Holländer,* but at 12:15 in the afternoon—one hour and forty-five minutes before air time—Miss Souvaine got a call from the Met: because of the indisposition of singers, the opera was going to be changed to *La Traviata.* Fifteen minutes later came another call: because of scenery problems, *La Traviata* was going to be changed to *Ariadne auf Naxos.*

This was a blow to Miss Souvaine. *Ariadne* had never been broadcast before. There was no script for Cross, no material in the files. By pure chance, two things were in her favor—the curtain was set for 2:30 instead of the usual 2 P.M., and, because *Ariadne* was scheduled for broadcast two weeks later, two tapes had already been recorded. The pre-broadcast analysis by Boris Goldovsky was ready to run. But the other tape, Opera News on the Air, which had John Gutman interviewing Maria Jeritza and Lotte Lehmann (the first singers to portray Ariadne and the Composer, respectively), ran an hour and had to be cut to twenty-five minutes.

At one o'clock, Miss Souvaine began working on Cross' script, which she presented to him ten minutes before he went on the air. At two o'clock, her assistant began work on the second part of Cross' script, and handed it over five minutes before intermission. Meanwhile, producer Souvaine had gone to work on the intermission tape (*Ariadne* has only one break): she had sixty-five minutes in which to hear *and* edit the sixty-minute recording. Standing by and ready to go on "live" if the editing could not be accomplished were the participants in the Opera Quiz, who had been scheduled for the original *Holländer* broadcast. Miss Souvaine never quite finished editing the tape, but it went on anyway and ran only a minute overtime. It was a job supremely well done, and the producer thankfully reports that it was the only time in her thirty-four-year history with the broadcasts that it *had* to be done.

The Met broadcasts, like so many of "the better things in life," rarely come in for any sort of serious criticism. It seems unfair to pick on a national institution that has consistently, for the past forty-two years, been offering 95 percent of the nation a chance to hear—free—a vital part of America's musical life. Surely, no one can argue with the broadcasts' record or the technical mode of presentation. The little carping that has taken place has always concerned artistic and aesthetic matters.

Rudolf Bing was particularly criticized for the choice of operas and casts that were assigned broadcast dates during his twenty-two-year regime. Geraldine Souvaine herself—no great fan of the former general manager—has suggested that "Bing took it for granted that people would listen, no matter what the cast." As a producer, Miss Souvaine, of course, wants only first-rate casts, or at least the same cast which appeared on the opening night of a production. As an example of what she means, Miss Souvaine cites the *La Fille du Régiment* broadcast, which was minus Luciano Pavarotti, who had a sensational success in his role.

Terry McEwen, classical manager of London Records, has a similar complaint. "Bing ignored the broadcasts," he says, "otherwise he wouldn't have put dogs on them, as he often did." McEwen also cites the existence of an "if they are singing at the Met, they must be good" attitude, which might have resulted in some careless casting. He further complains that "in the last ten years, there were many instances of new productions that were not broadcast until the following season."

Even Miss Souvaine and McEwen would have to admit that most of the great singers who have appeared at the Met over the years were also, at one time or another, given the privilege of singing on a broadcast. It must be understood, however, that a general manager has a problem on his hands when it comes to the broadcasts. Artists seek them out, often placing their value above that of an opening night. So the general manager has a powerful plum with which to bargain with singers. It becomes, then, a political game, and, as Geri Souvaine says, "There's already too damn much politics in opera." The producer feels that more competition would allow for less in-fighting and dirty politicking. She suggests that it would be interesting to see what would happen if the opera companies in San Francisco and Chicago began broadcasting nationally instead of locally.

Miss Souvaine has also come in for her share of bad notices. The intermission features vary only within a strict framework. There are those who believe that a change might allow for a much needed breath of fresh air. "There is a home-grown and corny quality about the intermissions which is not in tune with the country today," McEwen says. "On the other hand, that may be their charm. Look, I feel ambivalent about knocking the broadcasts. They're the single most important musical event in the country, and they've done more for music than anything else."

Probably the only thing about the broadcasts that has never received even the subtlest criticism is the long-standing sponsorship by Texaco. McEwen sums up that matter succinctly: "Texaco has done more for the Met than any general manager." Perhaps even Rudolf Bing wouldn't argue with him on that point.

Intermission

What opera might well have been subtitled Gong Busters?[1]
What operas besides Carmen *take place in Spain?*[2]
Who was Lohengrin's mother?[3]

THE QUESTIONS ARE AS ABUNDANT as snowflakes in a blizzard. Often they are as lightweight, sometimes as colorless and frequently as soggy. Each season a fresh truckload arrives. Listeners to Texaco's Opera Quiz never seem to tire. And they are optimistic. If their query is used on the air, they are rewarded handsomely by the famed "gift package"—four newly recorded operas and an AM-FM transistor radio.

The Opera Quiz is universally acknowledged to be the most popular intermission feature. Like all other spoken portions of the Met broadcasts, it is produced exclusively by Geraldine Souvaine. Neither the Met nor Texaco has any say in the format, choice of questions or choice of panelists. The post of quizmaster has been held since 1959 by Edward Downes.

Steady listeners know most of the regular panelists well. Miss Souvaine employs only a handful of them. The producer claims that she will try anybody with the proper credentials, but that only a half dozen or so have worked out well. Others, including a slew of music critics she once auditioned, suffered grievously from the worst sin on radio—mike fright.

[1] *Turandot.*

[2] *Don Giovanni, Le Nozze di Figaro, Fidelio, Il Barbiere di Siviglia, Don Carlo, Ernani, La Forza del Destino, Il Trovatore, Parsifal,* among others.

[3] Queen Konwiramur of Brobarsz whom Parzival (non-Wagnerian spelling) married in between his exploits at King Arthur's Round Table and his experiences at Monsalvat.

Among Miss Souvaine's favorite panelists are two men from the record world—John Coveney, artists' relations manager for Angel, and Terry McEwen, classical manager for London. The producer is particularly fond of Coveney's quick wit, and often cites a prize example. During the first broadcast from Lincoln Center, the quiz panelists were asked what they liked most about the new house. "Not seating latecomers," was Coveney's immediate reply. The next question was, what did they like *least* about the new house. "Not being able to get to my seat when I'm late," was the equally fast answer from Coveney.

Despite his humorous facility, Coveney takes his job seriously, and doesn't necessarily enjoy the ordeal. "I almost always come off with a headache," he reports. Over the years, however, he has learned to be less tense. People don't listen that closely, he has discovered, and frequently don't realize who gave which answer to what question.

Regular exposure on a national program, of course, makes the panelists celebrities of sorts. Once, while returning a rented car, Coveney was asked by a clerk, "Haven't I heard you on radio?" Terry McEwen can cite similar incidents, but claims that the most important result of his being on the quiz is its effect on his mother. "She's gotten a whole new standing in the community," McEwen says. "She's become the minor celebrity."

Coveney, McEwen and other panelists are generally invited to appear on the quiz about a month in advance. If they accept, they are asked to call Miss Souvaine's office not before 4 P.M. of the Friday before air date. They are then read anywhere from between four to eight discussion questions (they never hear the fact questions until the quiz itself). Friday night they are supposed to determine which of these they think are the most interesting. An hour or two before air time, they all meet to discuss their individual appraisals.

"I can't remember one quiz where we got to answer half of the questions we planned on," Coveney says. "We don't know what the fact questions will be, of course, and that's what keeps us on our toes and makes it stimulating."

The fact questions come and go, and are answered or not answered. It is the discussion questions that really get the panelists involved and give the listeners the most for their money. Once McEwen, in the heat of an argument with a fellow panelist, said that tenor Giacomo Lauri-Volpi "sang like an animal." As McEwen himself reports, "the adverse mail was unbelievable." Another time, McEwen announced that Rossini was his favorite composer. This too inspired enough pens to make the mailbags particularly heavy.

On another occasion, actor Tony Randall, a devoted opera-phile and frequent panelist, announced, in answering a question, that a masterpiece he didn't like was *Die Zauberflöte*. This caused the heavens to storm. And once the late critic Olin Downes, father of Edward Downes, couldn't answer the question about who Lohengrin's mother was, so he fliply remarked: "It must have been an immaculate conception." This crack proved to be more offensive than disliking Mozart.

Embarrassments and imbroglios aside, the quiz rolls merrily along and never seems to lose its popularity. Listeners whose questions don't get used one year try again and again the next. Since only one winning question per year per person is allowed, the fortunate ones also try their luck again in subsequent years. For those interested, questions may be submitted to: Texaco's Opera Quiz, Texaco, Inc., 135 East 42nd Street, New York, N.Y. 10017.

6

The First Year: Carmen

HE ELEVATED ORCHESTRA PIT, a mismatched mess of music stands and swivel chairs, virtually eclipses the chaotic proceedings on stage, where choristers listen to the piercing, accented voice of the gaunt, long-haired director. Leaping about like a choreographed demon, he attempts to show them where and how to stand. It is a tedious and repetitive business, but tempers are under control. Even the mighty principals are patient and good-humored.

The sole discord emanates from the stage manager who regularly barks a deep-throated warning that silence must reign supreme. Suddenly, from the wings, there appears an otherworldly vision—face haggard, hair askew, blazer on his shoulders, elegance in his bearing. "May I interject a musical comment? Is that allowed?" queries the unmistakable voice. "Please," replies the director graciously, falling exhausted into the nearest chair.

Leonard Bernstein has, for the nonce, taken over from Bodo Igesz, as the Metropolitan Opera's new production of Bizet's *Carmen* withstands yet another unscheduled interruption. But this is accepted as inevitable, and not in the least resented. These are no ordinary rehearsals. Not, perhaps, in the history of opera has one effort been plagued with the kind of tragic and troublesome crisis course as has this *Carmen*. When the opening-night curtain rises, the fact alone that it did so on schedule will be one of its foremost triumphs.

The trouble began long ago with, of all things, Wagner's *Tannhäuser,* the work Rudolf Bing bequeathed to Goeran Gentele to open his first season as general manager. Opera companies today must work two and three seasons ahead, so it was Bing's responsibility to chart the 1972–73 season, even though he was to have nothing whatsoever to do with its operation.

Gentele accepted *Tannhäuser* as a fait accompli until he discovered that the production was one of the seediest in the house. Quickly he set to work to remedy what has sometimes been dubbed "Bing's Revenge." He had to find not only another opera, but one that would suit the vocal talents of Marilyn Horne, James McCracken and Tom Krause, who had already been contracted for opening night. *Carmen* proved amenable to all, but then there arose another dilemma. The Met's production of the opera, while relatively new, was an unmitigated disaster. So Gentele went to his board and got the money for a new production. Bravely, and rather daringly, he assigned himself to direct the piece.

Everything seemed to be proceeding apace until the general manager, vacationing in Sardinia, was killed in an auto collision in 1972. Then all hell broke loose. Who would take over what was, in effect, a conception long in the planning and already completely designed? Rumors were rampant: Jerome Robbins would come in, or conductor Bernstein would stage it, in collaboration with designer Josef Svoboda. To the surprise of everybody, including himself, Bodo Igesz, a stage director at the Met since 1963, who was to assist Gentele, got the job.

The sinking ship was still in troubled water. Attempting to play from strength, acting general manager Schuyler Chapin replaced James Morris, the scheduled Zuniga, with Donald Gramm, a better-known commodity. Then, Teresa Stratas, the scheduled Micaëla, was ordered by her doctor not to sing for three months. She was replaced by Adriana Maliponte. Weeks before the premiere, Michael Tilson Thomas, who was to make his Met debut replacing Leonard Bernstein as conductor in later performances, withdrew.

When Schuyler Chapin phoned Marilyn Horne to tell her who the new director was, the baffled singer cried, "Bodo who?"

Both Miss Horne and Igesz laugh uproariously at this remembrance as they relax at the Met in the early evening following a strenuous day of rehearsing. In preparation for *Carmen* the mezzo shed some twenty pounds (her costar James McCracken shed ten pounds more than she did), and appears youthful and blooming, though still a mite chubby, in a long white skirt, blue print blouse, golden glasses and neat, cropped hair. Igesz, on the other hand, looks pinched and wan. His eyes are like sunken hollows in the head of a skeleton. "Bodo must weigh eighty-two pounds," Miss Horne says with concern.

Having never worked together before, both artists were initially wary of one another, but have overcome prejudices and now get along splendidly. They are aware of the ghost hovering over their ship. Igesz, for example, will receive credit for directing the production, but will have to contend with the handicap of its being "the Gentele conception." This, of course, lends an uncomfortable feeling to an atmosphere already crowded with diverse emotions. Igesz and Miss Horne had both talked at length with Gentele, thereby giving themselves the moral responsibility of upholding his ideas. They feel that an allegiance to some of these basic tenets is necessary, while total devotion to them would bring disaster.

"What we have on stage," Igesz explains, "is a set which has been designed with Gentele's conception in mind. Otherwise we have—I want to be very honest—some erratic things that we know he wanted. A point here, a point there, but that's all."

"He didn't have it all written down," Miss Horne adds.

"I have been trying like mad," Igesz continues, "to talk to people all over the world—Mrs. Gentele, Ragnar Ulfung, who was the Don José of the Stockholm production—trying to see which of Gentele's ideas we can use within the framework of the sets and within our possibilities. There are some thoughts Gentele had which I don't exactly understand. Therefore I don't think it right to use them on stage."

"Not only that," Miss Horne interjects, "Gentele also had said to me, we'll work things out in rehearsal. He knew that it was give and take with artists and the director. He never said, you gotta do this, or you gotta do that."

"Of course, there's a feeling of reverence," Igesz says, "but, on the other hand, if one tries to think too much—we have to stick to this, we have to stick to that—we'll end up with a museum piece, which is the last thing that Gentele would have wanted."

"Exactly," agrees Miss Horne, "and we'd all be tied up in knots."

Carmen will be the American singer's third role at the Met. She made her debut in 1970, as Adalgisa in *Norma,* and then went on to sing Rosina in *Il Barbiere di Siviglia.* Amsterdam-born Igesz, who is thirty-nine, has never before had his own production at the Met. In his capacity as stage director, he has assumed the productions of numerous directors who have long since departed.

Coincidentally, Igesz has, in the past two years, staged a trio of provincial *Carmen*s. Miss Horne's experience with the opera has been minimal—fifteen performances (in San Francisco, Philadelphia and Boston), not counting the dubbing she did for Dorothy Dandridge in the 1955 film, *Carmen Jones.* It is only of late that she feels her voice has developed enough to be suitable for the part.

Both artists are cognizant that of all operas in the standard repertory *Carmen* is the most popular and also the most difficult to bring off. Neither claims to have ever seen a truly successful interpretation, although Miss Horne thinks that Sarah Caldwell's Boston production, while under-rehearsed, worked as well as any she's ever been in or seen.

The mezzo is also quick to point out in her no-nonsense manner that not since Risë Stevens has New York had a Carmen who was thoroughly identified with the part. "I saw enough ads of Miss Stevens advertising Chesterfield cigarettes to have had a vision of Carmen," she recalls smiling, "but I never saw her do it. After I got into Carmen myself, I thought of her as a much wilder person—less of the marcelled-hair type."

"You know," Igesz interrupts, "I'm not referring to this cast, but there's no reason why either Carmen or José should be beautiful."

"Ha!" Miss Horne chuckles. "I was complaining to a friend of mine about my weight. 'Who ever said that Carmen was not supposed to be fat?' she said. I got news for you, I answered, she's not going to be thin!"

"Seriously speaking," Igesz continues, "there's no reason on earth, it's not written anywhere that she is beautiful. José couldn't explain why he was attracted to her."

"I also think she was a bit of a sorcerer," Miss Horne adds. "She had a lot of that witchcraft in her, and she really believed in the power of the rose and the power of the cards. Because she sees her destiny in the cards, it could be that she wills Don José to kill her. That's pretty strong stuff to put across on stage, though.

"*Carmen* is absolutely trapped in the middle of the nineteenth century. It is not verismo yet, and it is not of the bel canto period. But it is written as the first half of the nineteenth-century operas were—set arias, set duets, set trios, nothing else composed, obviously because of the spoken dialogue."

In the current production, part of the original Opéra-Comique dialogue—which over the years has been replaced by recitatives composed to different words by Ernest Guiraud—will be restored, in the hope of filling out the plot and giving it greater verisimilitude. "The story does live," Miss Horne says, "and we, living in the latter part of the twentieth century, have to make it extremely believable. *But,* it's got to be sung well, too. It needs a lot of style and vocal control. I think that for years certain Carmens have gotten away with screaming chest notes instead of really singing them. To do this role, you've got to have your voice in order."

Miss Horne would be happier if the dialogue were in English but realizes that at the Met, at least, this is a losing battle to engage in. Her tastes would also be more gratified if, instead of the stark and modern Svoboda sets, the scenery were lavish and realistic à la Zeffirelli. She had even discussed her partiality toward conventional stage design with Gentele, but was over-ruled. Particularly offensive to her in Svoboda's design is what she calls "the wall-to-wall, ceiling-to-ceiling carpeting. I'm not at all convinced that it isn't going to soak up sound. I'm very disturbed about it, and am trying to control myself."

Aside from the specifics of the carpeting, she realizes that the sets needn't necessarily be as only she envisions them. "I can conceive of other ways," she says easily, "and nobody would be happier than I if the whole thing comes off. I'm giving it all I've got."

Igesz feels much the same way, although he's in a very different position. "I must say, I feel surrounded by an incredible amount of support, help and goodwill—which hasn't always been the case in this house. I have a strong feeling that—if one talks to the chorus or to the soloists—one will find that there are many reasons for this. Not only Gentele's death, but the first production after a long time of suffering and God knows what else. That's one of the major things Gentele was able to do —change the complete mood and atmosphere of the house 100 percent. They were changes that were desperately necessary, too."

"When you think," Miss Horne exclaims, "that the man never really took over, he really had a strong influence." For Marilyn Horne, this should pose no problem. Either she makes it as Carmen or she doesn't. But Bodo Igesz almost can't win. "If the production is a success, credit, no doubt, will go to 'Gentele's conception.' If it's a failure, the fault will rest with me. That's only natural, I suppose, in this situation," he says realistically.

7

The First Year: Siegfried

HE NEW PRODUCTION of Wagner's *Siegfried* at the Met is not really new at all. It was built and ready to go on stage during the fall of 1969. What kept it in mothballs for three years involves a tale of assorted woes much akin to the misfortunes that plagued *Carmen,* the company's only other new production of the season. *Carmen,* however, is a parade of hit tunes, unlike Wagner's five-hour monster epic—possibly the composer's least popular opera.

The problems started when Rudolf Bing attempted to erect an Austrian/New York Axis by importing to the Met Herbert von Karajan's Salzburg Easter Festival conception of the four operas that embody Wagner's enormous *Der Ring des Nibelungen* cycle. This city had already gotten two installments—*Die Walküre* and *Das Rheingold*—when the Met's season was grounded by labor difficulties in 1969. Upon a belated resumption of activities, *Siegfried* had to be canceled because the principals, particularly maestro Karajan, were no longer available. For reasons no one is able, or willing, to explain, the Austrian music king wanted out. Suddenly the Axis Scheme collapsed, and the Met found itself with a Karajan Ring, but no Mr. Karajan.

It seems that for a while Bing sought a replacement. Impressed by Leonard Bernstein's success with a concert version of *Götterdämmerung* excerpts, the former general manager reportedly asked him to take over. By the time Bernstein supposedly said yes, Bing had decided to mount a new production of *Parsifal* in the time period allotted to a Ring opera. Another new Wagner production, *Tristan und Isolde,* followed last season. Still no *Ring.*

Enter Goeran Gentele who found himself stuck with this nasty unfinished business and, no doubt, pressure as well from Eastern Airlines, sponsor of the incomplete cycle. The late general manager moved quickly. Within weeks of his appointment, he phoned Erich Leinsdorf and asked him to come to the rescue. Leinsdorf accepted and everything seemed hunky-dory.

Then Gentele received a call from Kurt Herbert Adler, general director of the San Francisco Opera, who was asking a favor. In conjunction with the fiftieth anniversary of his company, might he keep Birgit Nilsson, Jess Thomas and Thomas Stewart for part of the time they were scheduled to be at the Met rehearsing *Siegfried,* and thereby run extra performances of the Ring? Obviously trying to be good-natured—but not carefully consulting his calendar—Gentele agreed. The upshot of the move was that the three principals did not arrive at the Met until only eleven days before the first performance of *Siegfried.*

This may have been for the best. There were yet touchy matters to be ironed out. Of all the people involved in the project, conductor Leinsdorf was perhaps in the most ticklish position. He had agreed to accept the musical responsibilities of a difficult work that came wrapped in a prepackaged conception—one that was conceived not by a director, but by a fellow conductor, Karajan. To add insult to injury, the scenic designer, Günther Schneider-Siemssen, had worked very closely with that conductor, and the director, Wolfgang Weber, had been his assistant. The veteran Leinsdorf hardly appeared perturbed.

"I am taking over *nothing*," he said firmly before the nitty-gritty rehearsals had begun. "I made this quite clear to Mr. Gentele. I am taking over three sets—not a concept. At one point, Mr. Schneider-Siemssen mumbled something about the fact that if we had any particular qualms, we could always have Karajan on the other end of the telephone wire. I immediately went to Gentele and said, look, if this is the case, then you had better find somebody else. Mr. Gentele said, and this is tragic, 'Let me assure you that I will be there. I have no reason to humor anybody who left the Metropolitan in midstream of a project.'

"Naturally, since the 18th of July [1972, when Gentele was killed in an auto accident] I have left the Met completely alone because they were harassed. The only thing I said was that Mr. Weber should be encouraged to follow his own mind. He will not be a representative of Karajan, of that I have been assured."

Those who assured him might have checked more carefully with Weber and his colleague Schneider-Siemssen. Both could not have been clearer in stating that they intended to re-create the general concept of the Salzburg/Karajan *Siegfried* for the Metropolitan. Speaking in German, which was translated by an interpreter, the designer said: "The person Karajan sends in his place, he trusts will carry out his plans the same way he would." Weber, whose English is better, agreed. "When Karajan asked me to do this, I said, why not? I know how each thought was created. I know him, and he knows me."

Speaking of Leinsdorf, Schneider-Siemssen said: "He is very fair. He said to me that he would speak to Karajan, and if Karajan had any special ideas or wishes, they would be carried out. I feel that this is proper when someone takes over, that he should check with the original concept."

Leinsdorf, when told of Schneider-Siemssen's impression, retorted: "Mr. Schneider-Siemssen wants to keep lines of communication open and doesn't want to burn his bridges. I don't blame him. When he suggested that Karajan could be available by phone, I nodded politely. I saw no point in telling him that I wouldn't dream of calling Karajan. The Metropolitan is not a branch office of any other opera company."

To confuse matters further, the three principal singers, reached by phone in California, were equally at odds. Said Jess Thomas: "Without being unduly modest, the three characters who carry the show until the third act are the Wanderer, Thomas Stewart, Mime, Gerhard Stolze, and Siegfried, myself. We have all done it with Karajan and will try to bring out his concept as much as possible. As far as Miss Nilsson is concerned—who has not sung in this production with Karajan—she's great. I'm sure she'll try to make the production what it was in Salzburg."

One wonders. Miss Nilsson has had a series of legendary rows with Karajan, and is not particularly disposed to his methods of working. Speaking of his absence, the Swedish dramatic soprano said sarcastically, "I'll try to survive, to overcome it. You know, I believe in having one man as conductor and another as stage director. To do both is not recommended. It's very worrying for us singers. There you are singing your soul out, and all of a sudden the conductor Karajan picks up the phone to tell an assistant that Nilsson has too much light on her face. This is not very inspiring."

Thomas Stewart also hoped for a new approach. "My wish is that we will go our own way," the baritone said. "We would do justice to ourselves—and maybe to Karajan too—if we would not try to stick to his conception. It's been too long since we did it in Salzburg—1969—and to remember it all from memory is a very tricky business."

All the singers spoke with great respect for Leinsdorf, with whom they had worked (as did Schneider-Siemssen) in the Met's 1971–72 hit production of *Tristan und Isolde*. The only problem is that no matter how deep a mark the conductor leaves on the work, it can only be temporary. Leinsdorf, by his own arrangement, is at the Met solely in a stopgap capacity to conduct *Siegfried* and *Walküre*.

"When Gentele approached me," the conductor recalled, "I said I'm delighted to be of help, but I don't want to continue to do Wagner and nothing but Wagner. Not that I'm tired of him, but once before, when I was a much younger man, I left the Met because I was pigeonholed. Also, I don't want to take on a Ring that is not really my baby. Of course, the whole thing was a misconceived project. I don't know why Bing went into this Karajan business."

Music Director Rafael Kubelik was to take charge of all the Ring operas, including a complete cycle in 1974–75, but resigned. Sixten Ehrling will complete the Ring. He, like Leinsdorf, will be stepping in rather than initiating, but the assignment will be less precarious. Even an entire Ring lacks the inherent difficulties of but one of its parts.

Leinsdorf explains why. "*Siegfried* has the same relative position to Wagner's other work that *Falstaff* has to Verdi's other work and *Gianni Schicchi* has to Puccini's other work. They are greater as compositions, but are lacking the highlights which make for the popularity of an opera. An opera is popular with a large crowd in proportion to its highlights. The composition can be the finest in the world. If the highlights aren't there, neither is the popularity."

As a totality, the Ring is chock-full of goodies, but they tend to come from the three other works, not from *Siegfried.* Pieces such as "The Entrance of the Gods into Valhalla," "The Magic Fire Music," "The Ride of the Valkyries," "Wotan's Farewell," "Siegfried's Rhine Journey and Funeral Music," "Brünnhilde's Immolation" and even the entire first act of *Walküre,* are relative staples and are frequently performed at concerts. But in all of *Siegfried* only the "Forest Murmurs" is performed in a concert arrangement.

Another reason for *Siegfried*'s unpopularity was suggested by Miss Nilsson. "There are too many male singers for too long a time," she said. "I'm not saying this because I'm a female singer. But two and a half acts with a lot of singing by Mime is too much. When he is good, it is wonderful, but very often you cannot get a good Mime." Miss Nilsson herself does not appear on stage until about 10:30 P.M. in *Siegfried,* which begins at 7. The only other female voices in the opera are those of Erda, who appears only in the third act, and the Forest Bird, who is heard briefly offstage.

All three principals feel that there are difficulties as well with their individual roles. "Somehow this is the most frightening of all the Brünnhildes," Miss Nilsson reported. "She is so exposed. I always feel that when I'm awakened from my long sleep, I am completely naked. You cannot act very much, and still you have to express three different sides of her character. She wakes up as a goddess. Then Siegfried starts to ask about his mother, and she says, 'I'll be your mother.' Finally her eyes are opened and she falls in love with him. Then she must become a woman. There's very little time to develop all of this."

Jess Thomas is in exactly the opposite position. "Siegfried is the longest role in opera history," he said. "People think of Hans Sachs and Gurnemanz as being longer, but they're nothing compared to Siegfried. I try to keep him young and light and avoid the heavyweight stuff. It's hard to interpret a character who doesn't know the meaning of fear. Siegfried is idealistic on the one hand, revolutionary on the other and, in a way, amoral. He's quite a study. Everything he does leads up to the great awakening in the third act—not only of Brünnhilde, but of Siegfried himself, both as a man and spiritually."

Thomas Stewart feels that "from the standpoint of a performer, Wotan, as the Wanderer, is the most interesting of them all. After this he never appears. You've worked your way through *Rheingold* and *Walküre* in developing the character, and have now arrived at the ripest point. The part is not as long as the one in *Walküre,* but histrionically it is more difficult and musically it's tricky."

That *Siegfried* is a tough work to put over, there is no argument. It is probably one of the few points on which Leinsdorf, Weber, Schneider-Siemssen and the singers concur. It seems a pity that with all this built-in liability, there had to be the added nuisance of an abandoned conception. Leinsdorf succinctly summed up the whole imbroglio: "This *Siegfried* is a foundling."

8

The Token Black
Who Paid Her Dues:
Leontyne Price

EONTYNE PRICE still smarts from the beating she took
battling her way to reach the twin-peaked summit where
she was crowned both prima donna *assoluta* and opera's
first black international superstar. The scars she carries
are invisible to the eye. But they become instantly evident
as the voluptuous and voluble diva explosively relives the stormier
portions of her life, those dulcet, mellifluous tones of hers taking
on a shrill, shrewish quality. This is the Price of today talking,
not the careful and polite, often cardboard figure of the past.

"My career was simultaneous with the opening up of civil
rights," the forty-six-year-old soprano says. "Whenever there was
any copy about me, what I was as an artist, what I had as
ability, got shoveled under because all the attention was on racial
connotations.

"I didn't have time then to fight back as an artist except to be
prepared and do my work and take that space because I was
the only person allowed the opportunity. That is what it meant
being black then. That is how much difference has been made
in a decade.

"I can feel the difference, and it is so wonderful even if you made the slightest contribution to it. That makes me feel just terrific, 'cause it means *survival*. It means you must have had what it takes. And to have enough left to go on is *fantastic!*" Miss Price exclaims, her voice cracking with emotion.

"I am just not afraid any more. I am not afraid to *fail*. And that makes things a lot better, because when you are a token black you can never allow yourself to even think in your subconscious that you can make a mistake. Talk to any black who's been in this particular palpitation and they'll tell you the same thing. You cannot afford *not* to burn the midnight oil longer than your colleagues, because in order to be heard you have to be infinitely more prepared. So that if you get in the door, you have to accept and almost gobble up everything that comes with it. With it, in my case, was pressure. I didn't even have time to lose my temper, to go through all the articles where wrong things were said.

"I think now I'm becoming whatever normal means again. I think I'm more professional, I'm growing up, I'm becoming a woman. It has done wonders for me vocally. Maybe freedom is just not being scared, and I'm *not* scared any more."

Between the year of her Met debut, 1961, and 1969, Miss Price gave 118 performances at the Met. Since then, she has appeared at the house quite infrequently. What has kept her away in recent years is an involved saga which reflects, better than anything, her current attitudes.

At the heart of the matter is ennui. With a mere two new productions under her belt, Miss Price is the undernourished darling of the company. Prima donnas require premieres the way lesser mortals need oxygen. Leontyne Price eventually found it more and more difficult to breathe in the Met's atmosphere. "I am not a very big temper-loser," she explains, "but I *have* a temper and it's the worst kind. I never throw things, but cerebrally I will get you off my back. And that's what I did. Very quietly, I told Mr. Bing I thought it was about time I got a rest from the Met.

"I told him it was not particularly exciting just to keep doing one *Aïda* and *Forza* after another, with never any real spice, any real impact. Granted, I will say completely immodestly that if I performed, I think there was certainly an artistic impact. That's my responsibility. But you like to feel a little

froufrou once in a while and get a little attention. If I don't
get it one place, I simply go and look for it someplace else.
If that makes my ego stand out, I guess it's about time."

Miss Price is also quick to relate that neither of her two new
Met productions was achieved with any great sense of pleasure.
"I really resent someone telling me that opening the new house
at Lincoln Center with *Antony and Cleopatra* was a favor,"
she sneers. "It was not only a tremendous responsibility, I earned
it by virtue of my work and ability. I still refer to the experience
as one of—survival of the fittest! And I got fed up with the attitude which I received from the former Met administration that
I had the plum of the century. That's *not* true, I had the plum
of responsibility."

The soprano's major bone of contention with *Antony* was
Franco Zeffirelli, whose million-dollar production of the Samuel
Barber opera was universally damned for completely overpower-
ing it, and whose costumes were criticized for being particularly
unbecoming to the star. Then, to add insult to injury, for her
next new production Rudolf Bing offered her *Il Trovatore,*
which was fine, but to be designed and directed by—you guessed
it—which was not fine at all. Eventually, Miss Price got her way,
and Zeffirelli was removed from the project, but the incident
left a terrible taste.

"It was colossal chutzpah of Mr. Bing to offer me that again,"
she snorts. "I mean, Zeffirelli's a genius, but I didn't want him
to be a genius for me twice in my operatic career. I think, shall
we say, that the love affair was beginning to be over at that
particular time. Anyway, I survived the Bing regime. And I
was certainly light and airy about starting things off freshly
with the new regime. But that feeling certainly isn't there right
now."

Miss Price's change of heart stems from the cancellation, for
reasons of economy, of the Met's new *Don Giovanni* production,
in which she was scheduled to sing Donna Anna in the spring
of 1974. Under normal circumstances, she might have been disappointed and irked, but considering her past rocky dealings
with the Met, she is simply resigned. 'I don't *have* to go there,"
she says. "And I don't have the slightest need to wring my hands
about whether the *Don Giovanni* is new or old. That is completely the truth. If I'm not happy at the Met, there are *innumer-*

able opportunities for me to be happy someplace else. Anyway, the amount of time that I intend to be at the Metropolitan will be just enough for me to be rosy. I don't wring my hands about anything anymore, except if I don't get eight hours' sleep. That's about where it's at for me now."

Unlike so many of her sister superstars, Miss Price has learned the lesson of never jamming her schedule. She leaves herself plenty of time in between performances, and always takes into consideration the rigors of jet lag. Because she is such good box office, her manager often has the frustrating task of having to say no to presenters who are forever eager for her services. The soprano picks and chooses as she pleases from among recitals and operatic and recording dates here and abroad.

"I am a very busy woman," she reports, "but it's done at my pace. Nothing is forced upon me. It is the type of freedom I would suggest every artist try to aspire to. It's absolutely fantastic, because I am in complete control."

It wasn't always so hunky-dory, nor was she always the mistress of her fate. On October 31, 1961, for example, Miss Price faced the humiliation of having to quit a Met performance of *La Fanciulla del West* after the second act. Her voice, tired from overwork and strain, just gave out. What followed was a grim period. But, after taking it easy for a couple of seasons, she bounced back in prime shape. The *Fanciulla* incident used to be a taboo subject chez Price; today, she'll gladly talk about it.

"You can't admit your failures until you really have room in yourself," she says. "That's pure objectivity when you can say, okay, I made a boo-boo and I won't do it again. That's very healthy, but you have to know when you can do it. For a long, long time after *Fanciulla,* if someone would just say *Fan . . .,* I would jump and immediately a curtain would be drawn. Now I don't. I couldn't care less. I've even recorded the aria. It was a kinda psychic thing, and now it isn't."

What actually happened? "I was running on two railroad tracks. It was overwork and being too many places at one time. I don't agree with everybody else when they say it was because of Puccini's orchestration. You know, I recorded *Carmen*. Everybody swore that did it, too. That's a lotta junk, dear, because sopranos have recorded *Carmen* before, and mine isn't really too bad. Actually, it's good. And I can't tell you how much fun we all had doing it. It never occurred to me *not* to do it. And then I get all this stuff afterwards about how if I had not recorded *Carmen* . . .

"I've just lately started laughing about all of this. It all comes down to what people think you ought to do with a certain sound, and they won't give that up for any reason at all. That's what's so wonderful about having a voice—the reaction of people, which I think is so beautiful. For instance, if there's someone who, as the kids say, digs your sound, they sort of take it and it becomes theirs. Every time they come to hear you, if you do anything which is not what they think that sound should be, they get completely and personally offended by it. Even if you succeed at it, they think, well, okay, you made it this time, but maybe you wouldn't the next time. It's kinda fun; they really possess your sound.

"Anyway, at that point in time, Minnie was not the right thing to do. I wasn't the world's greatest Tatiana in *Eugene Onegin,* or Fiordiligi or Thaïs either. That's about it, though."

While Miss Price is open to criticism and will often supply it herself, she is the first to admit that there is a time and place for such matters. In her dressing room following a performance is neither. "It's a trip to perform," she says, relishing the subject, "and if you make it, whether it's good or bad, you're already on a cloud somewhere out there. And nobody's out there with you, except the people who took the same trip. I always tell my manager and friend, Hubert Dilworth, don't bring anybody in my dressing room who is not going to tell me that I am the most glorious thing they ever heard, because I don't want to waste my time. That is just a general rule. Now Hubert can't always check that out, but there's something about my attitude that makes people know that is not the time to be critical. I have actually said this: If you don't tell me I'm magnificent, then go straight home with your ticket stub immediately. This is not the place for you."

Miss Price shakes with laughter as she recalls the unfortunate soul who once made the mistake of his life backstage with her. "It was after a recital in some town," she says. "There was this gentle_____ who just started waving at me from way down at the end of the line. I thought, well, if nobody else really dug my performance—and I really thought I was on—he did. It's just a matter of putting up with the rest of these people till he gets to me. I thought, my goodness gracious, another fan won! So he gets up to me and he says, 'Miss Price, did I detect a slight strain on your B-flat in the aria?' I said, smiling all the time, 'Would you do me a small favor and get quietly out of the line so the other people can tell me beautiful things about my B-flat.' I really was a little rougher than that, but I can't tell you what I said. I was so furious with that man! My first impulse was to smack him in his head, but I relinquished that strong desire. I'll never tell what I said to him. It was *bad*—straight to the jugular vein."

The new Leontyne Price who has given up tippy-toeing on eggshells all the time, both publicly and privately, is able to confront the simple but difficult question, "Where do you stand among sopranos today?" At first she is amusedly nonplussed and cracks, "You're out of your mind. That is an impossible question!" Then, she ponders it for a while and finally says, minus any coyness, "on the crest of the wave, the crème de la crème."

In such a position, she is able to be charitable about her colleagues, a trait most sopranos find alien to their characters. Actually, she speaks with great respect of a number of her fellow artists. "From a purely technical point of view, there are three singers who are unsurpassable. They are Madames Sutherland, Horne and Sills. I am also a great admirer of Madame Caballé, from a technical and dramatic point of view.

"I don't know quite how to express this, but I relate to Madame Tebaldi so much. There's something so moving in her voice—a warm, human accent that I enjoy immensely. Histrionically on the stage today, I think there is one artist who is absolutely unbeatable, and that is Madame Grace Bumbry. She is the most electric thing that has happened theatrically in many a decade. I have great respect for her.

"Madame Schwarzkopf, particularly from a recital point of view, is someone I think I've learned a great deal from. I mean the delivery, the whole ambience she expresses in chamber music, is something I think we could all aspire to. Of course, *numero uno* for me, who I think has given us all the ultimate gift, is La Callas. She really got the ball game going."

The more she talks, the more Miss Price relaxes until she

is completely at ease seated on a couch in the living room of her south Greenwich Village twelve-room, Federal-era house. She is quite striking in a bright, multicolored Chuck Howard pantsuit, huge, golden loop earrings and an enormous and becoming Afro. She is a woman of ample proportions, warm, feminine, gracious and extremely outgoing.

And yet, despite the almost legendary status she has enjoyed since hitting the big time in this country in 1961, Miss Price has come under fire in some quarters for being rather haughty, arrogant and grand. She has also been described as having a constantly fluctuating dual personality. One moment she's a down-to-earth woman with a tangy sense of humor, the next she's a forbidding and regal prima dona. Like so much else about her, this is a misconception.

"Nobody believes me, but I'm so shy, most of the time I really don't know quite what to say. And if I don't know what to say, I won't say anything at all, which gives people the feeling that I'm away from it all and aloof. I'll act as if I'm in complete control, but it's usually because I'm scared to death. I'm very uncomfortable with froufrou French waiters going around me. They make me nervous. I feel terribly self-conscious being in the right place at the right time in the right dress. I only have enough chutzpah to be in the right place on stage. That's where it's at for me."

Her fears and her resultant play-acting have even cost her some friends, particularly at the start of her career when there was little time for anything but work. She is now trying to re-establish some of these lost connections and is discovering "a backlash. They are being a little aloof with me, because they were hurt. I had no idea I was giving off the impression of being Miss Hoity-Toity."

Although she currently has more time for her personal life, Miss Price is not shopping around for a husband. One matrimonial whirl (to baritone William Warfield), which ended in divorce, proved sufficient for her. "If you get used to receiving love, warmth and emotion from three or four thousand people, it's a little tricky for one person to give it to you. You're lucky if you can find a man who can handle that." Has she found him? "Do you mean, am I involved with someone?" Miss Price asks with mock coyness. "Of course. How can you function without being involved? I would die; that would make me abnormal. I just don't want to get legally bound, that's all."

Miss Price has also come under fire because of her less than militant stance on the black issues. "My involvement was being black, not talking about it," she snaps. "I think when you don't say much, people think you're not saying anything. Why should I sit around chatting when I'm busy getting things done?"

Although she feels a kinship with them more in general than in specific terms, Miss Price is a great admirer of the Black Panthers. "There was a lot of attention drawn to the black front by these militants," the diva says. "They weren't afraid to say, look, we want to stand up and be counted. The ultimate aim is to be heard. They didn't tippy-toe around. Having tried to come into that area of courage, I'm grateful to them because I think it's brought something out in me. I don't know anything about the hypertechnical rules of the party, but I agree with the philosophy of shaking people to listen to blacks."

The soprano would like to do more than shake the press, which she feels is responsible for yet another misunderstanding, and one that really hurt: The fiction that it was the wealthy Chisholm family in her hometown of Laurel, Mississippi, and not her parents, who gave her most of the financial and moral support she needed as a young woman. "Don't get me wrong now," she says heatedly, "the Chisholms are really good people. They're lovely people. But what I'm trying to put in context is something even they will admit: They received exposure because of the racial angle.

"It was more newsworthy to accent financial aid from a white family than to acknowledge that my parents were my parents. I *hate* the very idea that it looked like my parents were in the wings and the Chisholms were onstage, because it is an *undiluted* lie. There was more attention paid to that than almost to what I was singing. It was wrong. But the Chisholm legend was made by the press, not by Leontyne Price."

Both Miss Price's parents are dead—her father died in 1968, her mother in 1972. The daughter speaks of her mother with a love so warm and real, it becomes almost something you can touch. "She was an incredible woman. There never was and never will be another like her. She did pretty good. I've got a brother who is a brigadier general. When he was a colonel, he was the first black division chief of staff in the history of the U.S. Army. He's some Tarzan, that one. He's the real star of the family.

"I always say it's mama who gets me onstage. She had fire to burn. She has always been my strongest source of inspiration. The cord was really just cut. I'm not even ashamed to admit that I was immature enough to call her before I left home for a performance. There was an element of calm about her. I always knew that with her I didn't have to prove anything that night. Maybe that's why I called her.

"I'll never forget when I was home in 1972. She was waking up from a nap and I was right there. I think that meant something to her. I didn't want someone else to be there. I was there myself. She said, 'You're not canceling anything, are you?' I said, 'Yes, I'm not going to do the *Forzas*.' She said, 'Oh, yes, you are! Promise me you're not going to cancel one single thing.' I promised her. She said, 'You'll be all right.' And I really was. It just kinda shaped me up. That's been her idea all the time. Also, she always said, 'If you can't be first, get out of the ball game.' I'm a fanatic about that. I can't stand to be second at anything. Isn't that awful?"

Leontyne Price listened well to her mother. "As a token black, I paid my dues. I realize that because I am black, I will still always be on kind of a duty. There are still many things that have to be done. It is kind of wonderful, though, that they're divided in half. That's the kind of elasticity I'm living through now. To be able to concentrate on being a plain singer, without the overwhelming weight of the monkey on your back. I think it has been lightened, not completely pulled together, but lightened. I want to take advantage of that particular lightness.

"I can't live without *speranza*—hope. I mean that not only artistically, but *en général*. I mean, to be able to recognize that there's still a sense of direction, but that some of the plowing is finished with. It's like planting crop kinda time. That may be a provincial way to put it, but I think I know what I'm talking about. It's kind of wonderful: you have the anticipation of something really sprouting out. This is an inkling of how I feel just being a human being first, without any monkeys on my back. It's just a taste but, my God, it makes you want to eat an awful lot."

9

Queen of the Wagnerians:

Birgit Nilsson

IRGIT NILSSON, fifty-five years old, is a hefty and powerful former farm girl who is not given to fear nor easily intimidated. In fact, there is probably only one thing capable of transforming this intrepid Queen of the Wagnerians into a very unregal bundle of nerves, and that, strangely enough, is a New York recital.

"Ah, every time is a nightmare," the soprano groans in her malaproped, Swedishized English. "I'm an opera singer. That is my real field. In an opera, you have costumes, an orchestra, other colleagues. The whole evening is not dependable on you. In a recital, you feel you are absolutely naked. You stand there with a pianist and a piano, and there you are. You have to create twenty different moods. In an opera, you are creating only one role.

"I'm out of my mind every time. And before I have the program done, I go like a hen who wants to lie an egg and cannot find a place. Oh, and I say to myself, why do I promise to sing in New York? Oh, oh. It's fun, but it's so hard."

The dramatic soprano is garbed in an ordinary hausfrau mock turtleneck sweater and skirt and is comfortably hugging a couch corner in her New York apartment hotel. If she is not quite living up to her reputation for being the funniest soprano alive, she is surely the giggliest. Almost anything is capable of setting her off on a volley of unending laughter. But this is her sole indulgence. Otherwise, she is remarkably still and patient during a long interview. Her only movement as she expansively chatters and giggles nonstop is to tuck one or both of her shapely gams beneath her rear.

Stillness and patience be damned, Nilsson shrieks with laughter when asked if, like tenors, sopranos have to be careful about their sexual activity before singing. "I know a story about a tenor," she says, avoiding the question at first, "who finally found a girl and they were in bed when the telephone rang. He said, oh, I see, yes, yes, of course, good-bye. 'Dress, we have to dress,' he told the girl. 'I'm singing Tristan in three months.' "

But what about sopranos? "No, I don't think so—for sopranos. Haven't you heard about the famous soprano at the Met who took a tenor who was making his debut into her dressing room before the performance and they had an affair? He made a big flop and she stole the evening. Very cruel. I think it's the tenors who have to be careful."

Speaking of tenors, have she and Franco Corelli—one of the few leading men capable of matching Nilsson's stentorian tones decibel for decibel—stopped feuding? There was a period when it looked as if their heroic squabbles might make the history books. "It was only in the beginning," Nilsson says, obviously relishing the subject and already starting to laugh. "I'm always good friends with all my colleagues. But, you know, two strangers, before they know each other's temperament and so on, one holds the high note longer than the other one. I'm sure he succeeded most of the time. But the time I succeeded, he got very mad at me."

Nilsson is referring to one occasion when Corelli refused to continue a performance of *Turandot* because she held a high note in a duet longer than he did. "The audience loved it; it was like a bullfight." Nilsson giggles. "In this scene, of course, he has the long rest. I'm singing the aria, and he just comes in at the end.

"Once, I almost forgot the cue and the music and everything. It was a broadcast at the Met, and I don't know how I ever came over it. At one point, Franco stands with his back to the public and I sing to him. All of a sudden, he puts his hands down into his panties and feels around. I kept looking at what he's doing, at what is going to happen. Suddenly, he comes up with a sponge

which he sucks and gives to the chorus lady who is sitting near
him. I laughed so hard inside when I saw it—I had to keep my
face straight—I thought I would never come over it.

"Franco, you know, always has a dry throat, so he keeps
sponges and glasses of water all over the stage. He wants to be
really fit for the high C's. He stands and prepares himself all
the time while I sing my head off. Then when the C's come, he
just turns around and goes down to the prompter's box and belts
out those incredible big tones which only he has. He must have
iron lungs because he holds them for hours—or it seems like
hours to me.

"In his heart of hearts, he's a good man, a very nice person.
He has an Italian temperament, and he wants so much to give
his best. That's why he worries so much. A good artist is always
nervous. He's *very* nervous."

Birgit Nilsson has come a long way from the provincial singer
who made her operatic debut in Stockholm in 1946 as Agathe in
Der Freischütz. Friends say she has not mellowed much; rather,
through experience she has grown wiser. She is still marvelously
adept when it comes to the quick, killing retort, but she is hardly
the same soprano who once left London in a huff because a critic
there complained that she was not yet the perfect Brünnhilde
("If I'm not perfect, let them find someone who is," was her exit
line). Nilsson herself admits to few changes in her personal
makeup ("I'm a simple person from the country"), and close
friends agree with her. But to a stranger it appears that there
has been a melting of some of the Nordic ice that once froze
her into a replica of the Princess Turandot she so realistically
interprets.

The soprano has had what is probably a record of 119 new
productions mounted for her by the major opera companies of
the world. The number itself is as staggering as the repertory
is diverse and demanding: 13 new Ring cycles, 10 new *Turandot*s,
5 new *Fidelio*s, 5 new *Salome*s, 7 new *Elektra*s, 4 new *Aida*s and
22 new *Tristan*s. The Metropolitan alone has staged two new
productions of the Wagner opera for her, the latter proving to
be one of the greatest triumphs of her career.

This unusually wide exposure to the world's greatest theaters,
directors and conductors has given the soprano the perspective
to arrive at a theory that is typically Nilssonian. She compares

an earlier era when prima donnas were supposed to have reigned supreme to today, when "we are the ones who have to adjust ourselves to the conductors, stage directors, designers. They have so much power. We are not allowed to have our own approach to a role. We have to have ten different kinds of approaches.

"I have sung Isolde close to two hundred times. Yet a conductor comes to me and says, 'I know I'm right,' and in the first act he drags it out for ninety minutes when I am used to singing it in seventy-three or seventy-five minutes. If he refuses to follow me, what can I do? I hate to throw a tantrum if I don't have to. I have to get a completely other approach. But I don't like singing the first act of *Tristan und Isolde* this way, I'm sorry."

Usually Nilsson will try to meet a prima donna conductor halfway. There is one maestro, however, with whom she won't even talk turkey let alone perform, and that is the superstar of them all, Herbert von Karajan. She has had a history of nasty contretemps with the Austrian music director, including one incident in which, following a rehearsal of one of his notoriously dark productions, she donned a miner's helmet to which she added not only a lantern but the traditional Valkyrie wings. Nilsson, when she chooses to squabble, picks opponents her own size, and when it comes to Karajan, the diva is raring to go.

"I still don't think he himself knows how wrong he is in his productions," Nilsson says seriously, "because he doesn't see them at the end. Of course, nobody appreciates his work as a stage director; that we all know. I mean he's a great conductor, and he has all my respect. But as a stage director, when he makes all those light rehearsals, or dark rehearsals, he doesn't count on the fact that the orchestra pit is not lit. When the performance comes, he brings the pit up higher, you can see him from the knees up, and he has a spotlight on him, of course.

"The public gets all the light from the orchestra pit in their eyes. And the stage remains dark. It's insane; and nobody dares to tell him because they're afraid of him. This is the way Karajan feels he is great—that he has the power and nobody is worth anything around him."

Karajan's insistence on conducting without a score, a habit which has influenced a generation of younger musicians in awe of the maestro, is also one of the soprano's pet peeves. But she doesn't reserve her disdain solely for von Karajan. "It is so unnecessary to conduct without a score," Nilsson says. "You know, we are only human, we can get a blackout, and when it happens we are left without help. They also can get lost. There are three very famous conductors who go without the score who got lost in performances I was singing. It was absolutely terrible.

"In a *Tristan,* I got a blackout and looked at the conductor. He was lost, too, and started to look at the musicians and pretend that he was very preoccupied with them. And the prompter! He didn't know what to do! We have great conductors like Böhm and Solti who never leave the score. Szell and Knappertsbusch didn't either. They always asked Knappertsbusch why he didn't conduct without a score and he said, 'Because I can read music.' "

Mistress of the one-liner herself, Nilsson is particularly fond of this retort and shakes with laughter. The soprano is always on the level; what she has to say is for the record. There is none of the coy, off-the-record bitchery common among some of her colleagues. Nilsson herself would probably claim that her direct approach stems from the Swedish national character and from her modest background.

As much as she insists on this image of herself, and as valid as it is up to a point—Nilsson is really earthy in the true sense of the word—even she will admit that being an international superstar makes extraordinary claims upon one. "You know, if you are somebody," she says rather sadly, "there are always those people who want to live through you. They have a certain way of trying to grab at your life which irritates one and makes one very impatient. On the other hand, I also get very annoyed when I feel I'm unfriendly to people. Sometimes I *am* unfriendly —then I suffer so much after. Ahhh, it's so hard to find the right way.

"If you are a little bit too friendly, they want to possess you. If you are a little bit unfriendly, you feel uncomfortable yourself and feel you are maybe hurting somebody. On the other hand, when I think, my God, I don't have time to write my own father, or I don't have time for my own family, just for these people who won't know me as soon as I can't sing good anymore—they won't even remember my name—it's a very, very hard thing to manage. I know there are artists who close themselves and who couldn't care less. I cannot lock myself up. I just cannot ignore. Sometimes I pay too much attention to people which keeps me from giving my best in my work. Whatever you do is wrong. It's an incredible conflict."

It's one of the few in a basically unconflicted career which has been handled with the kind of cool intelligence that allows Nilsson to observe the future realistically. "Many times when I am home in Sweden for a week or ten days, I think it is stupid to go on because I cannot probably achieve any more than I already have," she says. "On the other hand, it's wonderful when I start again, and it's rewarding when I find new things in a song which I wasn't able to do before.

"Of course, it cannot go on forever. I'm very well aware of that. It can maybe happen overnight. You wake up and say, I don't feel like singing anymore, the voice is not so. I don't know. If I would all of a sudden feel that things are not going as well as they should, there would be absolutely no use to go on."

With all her levelheadedness, Nilsson still finds it difficult to follow one of her own mottoes: "The most important thing in our business is to learn to say no," she says with a resigned smile that implies little luck in such endeavors. It is the public who reaps the rewards of her weakness. For example, although she has been consistent in her claim that she will not broaden her repertory, there are some changes—good and bad—to report.

In concert form, she may sing Ariadne, and either the Empress or the Dyer's Wife in *Die Frau ohne Schatten*. Her inability to choose between the two latter roles has caused her problems. She was offered the Dyer's Wife in the Met's production of the Strauss opera, but turned it down because at that point she felt that only the Empress suited her (Christa Ludwig went on to sing the Dyer's Wife with tremendous success). Today, Nilsson tends to favor the role of the wife.

The bad news is that Nilsson will no longer be singing Salome. "Here in America," she says, "they expect a Salome who is eighteen or twenty years old. And the dance is the most important thing. The way *Salome* has been reviewed here, I just think it is better to stay away from it. People are listening with their eyes too much."

Although there are no other scheduled repertory changes, Nilsson has been having dreams which will set the Freudians aflutter. "I may be too realistic to think about this," she relates, "but it very often happens to me that I dream I sing roles I don't know very well. Very often it's Carmen. Maybe it's in the back of my mind.

"You know, when Goeran Gentele was a stage director in Stockholm, he tried to convince me to sing Carmen. He made my first Salome. Without him I don't think I could have done it. He worked every step with me, and the results were absolutely marvelous. The next opera he was to stage was *Carmen,* but there was no one to sing it. He called me every morning for three weeks and tried to convince me. I said, no, no. But I very often dream that I have to sing it. It's a terrible nightmare."

Well, why not sing Carmen? "Oh, no, no, no." You can sing it, can't you? "I can! I can! But how?" The Nilsson giggle can probably be heard as far as the Met, where they can use a good laugh.

10

The Old Guard:
Richard Tucker and
Robert Merrill

I N AN ATMOSPHERE charged with gags, raucous laughter and slaughtering of the Queen's English, two Runyonesque cronies named Richard Tucker and Robert Merrill are reminiscing. Behaving not the least like distinguished elder statesmen of the operatic arts, they come on more like veterans of the vocal wars who still have a few good battles to fight. Tucker, in particular, lets off steam by the bucketful as he alternates between playing pundit and *pagliaccio*. In the former guise, he points to my tape recorder and solemnly announces, "You can hold this for posterity, ya know." I suppose he is right because both men are legends in their own time. As paragons of vocal longevity, they are secure in their positions, more than willing to share the secrets of their success and not averse to offering advice to young warriors. The problem is, they haven't found too many takers.

Why won't the big-shot fledglings listen to the pros? Listen to baritone Merrill: "There was a young bass at the Met—I won't mention his name—who was doing very well. He was talented, musical as hell, good-looking and had a beautiful voice.

Then they gave him Escamillo, a role generally for a baritone. It was a new production and he looked Spanish. The first performance was good, but I found that he was singing within limits. So I walked over to him, because I liked him very much, and said, 'Try not to do Escamillo right now. I know you can get away with it, but save it for later. Pinza tried and he quit.' The bass looked at me sideways and said, 'Why? You worried?' After that crack, I told myself I'll never interject anything again unless I'm asked."

Less afraid of naming names, tenor Tucker puts it straight on the line: "I like this boy Placido Domingo very much. Not that he's ever told anybody, but he owes his life to me. Why? 'Cause I got him into the Metropolitan Opera, that's why. Nobody knows this. They needed a tenor to replace me in a performance, and I said there's a boy next door at the City Opera, get him. Bing and his assistants had called Domingo provincial. Everything in life is timing. I also gave him his La Scala debut in *Ernani,* which I turned down. One day at rehearsal I met him and said, 'Placido, you wanna go to Scala? Send them a telegram and tell them you're available in December.' You think he ever thanked me?

"His record contract—look what it cost me. Why? 'Cause I had an argument with RCA who wouldn't let me leave Rome in the middle of a recording session to attend my first grandson's circumcision. What grandfather wouldn't go home for this? I left and was back in two days, but it cost me my entire contract. Then they engaged Domingo. Today he's their fair-haired boy.

"And what is he singing now? Everything from *Traviata* to *Otello.* Young singers today have gotta learn to say no. Later on they'll reap the benefits. How many careers have shot their so-called thing in five years? It's because of the wrong repertory."

Tucker and Merrill practice what they preach. The tenor didn't sing *Pagliacci* until his twenty-fifth year at the Met; the baritone didn't do Scarpia until fifteen years after his debut. Of course, the tenor voice killer of all time, Otello, is a role Tucker won't touch, even for records. "Only fools, idiots, sing it," he says hotly. "With respect to my colleagues Jonny Vickers and Mc-Cracken, they can't sing legato any more. The best proof is Del Monaco. He was a great Otello, but once when I met him in Verona, you know what he said? 'You're the smart one. *Io*

stupido!' He couldn't sing legato any more. Even better proof is that Caruso never sang the role."

More than a quarter of a century ago, within nine months of one another, Tucker and Merrill, two boys from Brooklyn whose names then were Reuben Ticker and Moishe Miller, became overnight stars of the Metropolitan Opera. Each in his particular category has since nourished the company. They have had their detractors, but even the toughest critic could hardly deny the fact that they have served the Met well and with a consistent standard of artistry few singers of the past can match. Most extraordinary is that Tucker at fifty-nine and Merrill at fifty-four are still going strong, at the Met and elsewhere.

There is no doubt in anybody's mind that Tucker and Merrill are graduates cum laude of the don't-stint-on-the-volume school of singing. They've always blasted out notes so that they could be heard in the last row of the family circle. In fact, they've been criticized for this, Tucker in particular. It comes as a shock, then, to hear the tenor complain that "bel canto today is completely dead. Opera singers are only concerned with one thing—being heard. All you hear now is bellowing, forte, nothing with a legato line."

Subtlety has never been their thing—onstage or off. Sprawled on a couch in Tucker's Central Park South home away from home (both live in the suburbs), their air of amiability and joviality, their jokes and their laughter lend a nightclub aura to the surroundings. They are both sporting nifty glen plaid suits, boots and flashy accessories. Jackets are off, ties are loosened. Merrill, as spare as his buddy is stout, is quite the dude in a bright blue-green striped shirt and a tie that's fuchsia on black. Their ornate garb coordinates perfectly with the ornate decor. Affluence is evident everywhere.

Like all old-timers, the singers enjoy swapping stories. They have steamer trunks full of amusing anecdotes, and are willing to tell them nonstop. Each is the other's best audience.

"I'll never forget singing *Forza* with Eileen Farrell, one of my all-time favorite sopranos," Merrill says, already laughing. "God blessed her with large breasts. One time, during a dress rehearsal, she stood over me and her breasts kept falling in my face. There I am dying and I can't do a damn thing. So I asked her if she's got a cookie to go with the milk. On opening night, she brought me one."

Tucker, almost felled by spasms of laughter, screws up the strength to tell of the *Carmen* rehearsal with the late Fritz Reiner conducting when the stage manager sent him out late and he missed a cue. "Reiner stopped the orchestra and started hollering, "What's the matter with that tenor, what's the matter with Tucker?' I said, 'Maestro, don't holler at me! You got a guy back here who don't know the music.' He said, 'What do you want me to do with this stick?' I said, 'Stick it!' After the rehearsal, Reiner's wife came back to my dressing room, kissed me, and from that moment on I became her favorite tenor."

Toscanini, Mitropoulos, Cleva—name the conductor and they've got the story. There's one incident Tucker revels in relating, although it isn't funny. "I've been one of the artists who has a sincere feeling for our Jewish people," he says seriously. "When I discovered that Herbert von Karajan would be conducting my first two recordings at La Scala with Callas in 1953, I protested. He was a Nazi, you know. I said to the producer, 'Do you realize what this will do to me in America? My Jewish people will kill me.' I went to very far extremes, like sending cables to the World Jewish Congress in London. They wired back in the affirmative, that Karajan had been a member of the Nazi party.

"So I told EMI, either get yourself a new tenor or a new conductor. Now, how many singers would relinquish such an opportunity? I can honestly tell you that it cost me over a quarter of a million dollars in recording royalties because after the first two albums, which were conducted by Serafin, I was dropped like a hot potato. When I finally made my debut at the Vienna Staatsoper, von Karajan wouldn't conduct for me, naturally, but he had the courtesy to come to my dressing room, and with that Germanic clicking of the heels said, '*Kammersänger* Tucker, welcome,' and walked right out. He was a gentleman, which I admire, but he never forgot what happened and I don't blame him."

Tucker's recording career has been jinxed from the start. In the forties, he signed an exclusive contract with Columbia, a company which has never been opera oriented. As a result of this commitment, he has made few complete opera albums, except as a farm-out on other labels. Merrill, on the other hand, spent eighteen happy years with RCA, and at one period had four pages in their catalogue.

"It was the biggest mistake of my career," Tucker says. "You know, a young artist sees money thrown in his face and he's elated. Don't forget, when I contracted with Columbia, I was one of the few artists—with respect to Bob or anyone else—who had signed a six-figure contract with the Met in their first year. Now, this was unheard of. But with records, I was like a ballplayer being paid to sit on the bench. Here I had a contract and they weren't makin' any operas. The only thing I was doing was my own albums, which was good enough, but not good enough for my career later."

For Tucker, this and perhaps his not having made a film or two are the only areas he feels he mishandled in an otherwise busy and lucrative life in music. Merrill claims to have no qualms about the path his career has taken. Neither has any grounds for complaint. Their colleagues and competitors have come and gone; they're still here. Have they given any thought to calling it quits themselves?

"Lemme tell you something," Merrill says. "Years ago, Richard Tucker said that when he turned fifty he would quit. Even then, I told him, you won't. He didn't—and that summarizes the whole question. As far as I'm concerned, I'm gonna work until I stop enjoying it."

"I don't believe in the malarkey of enjoying," Tucker interjects. "When I said I'd quit at fifty, I was much younger and didn't realize that the years were going to pass so fast. I have corrected my previous statement, and what I said I still maintain: When Richard Tucker cannot give the best of Richard Tucker, that's when I quit. The mental strain on a person like myself or Bob standing on a stage is tremendous. You cannot sing an opera transposed down two, three tones. When my B-flats don't have security, that's it."

Merrill appears deep in thought. "That's what I meant," he says. "You can only enjoy something when you're doing it well. If I'm going to worry about making it every night, I'll quit. I just hope I have the courage, the strength of character, to do it. A lot of artists in the twilight of their careers must have said what we're saying. Some of them retired, some of them didn't."

"Who can ever forget the last Callas performance of *Tosca*?"

Tucker says. "She had the miserable misfortune of cracking on the high C in the third act, and the Tebaldi fans were out there booing. But Callas was a real pro. When the curtain came down, instead of freezing and not taking a bow, she said to me, 'Come, Richard, they love us.' "

"Yeah," Merrill says sadly. "But I have the feeling that when she went home, she was concerned about it. She didn't go out and celebrate. I know how I feel when I've had a bad night. I can't wait to get off the stage. I'm miserable."

Merrill reports that even today, when he is doing something new or important, he is often frightened for as long as two months before the performance. He considers himself lucky that for the past thirty-nine years he has had the security of being able to study with the same voice teacher. Tucker has been less fortunate; his voice teacher died.

"I still wanted to continue studying," Tucker says. "For two years I went from studio to studio, but nobody would take me. This is the honest truth. Look, I told them, I don't wanna learn nothing new, just tell me if the voice is going back in my throat. Correct it, that's all. One after another, they said, 'Richard, I understand what you want, but the minute you stop coming to see me, the rest of the studio will walk out thinking I'm not good enough for Richard Tucker.' It was idiotic."

These are the vicissitudes of stardom. But, as Tucker himself says: "If an artist is sincere, like Bob and I are, we strive for perfection. We never look back. We go ahead."

This double exposure of Placido Domingo and Sherrill Milnes was taken over a period of a month and a half because there was no way of photographing the busy singers together during the period I was working on this book. Domingo, on the left, was photographed first, with Milnes placed on each frame later. The entire roll of 35mm film was exposed for Domingo, taken out of the camera, and six weeks later put back into the camera for the second image, Milnes. The film leader was marked with a felt pen so that the film placement was exact both times. No tripod was used, although the distance from camera to subject was noted in the first session so that the second sitting could be set up the same way. Both men were asked in advance to wear black turtlenecks, and the room in which the pictures were taken was completely dark. The lighting source was a 75-watt light bulb. Exposure was f4 at one-sixtieth of a second.

Pictures of this kind are great fun to make because of the unpredictability of where each image will appear on the film—one of the reasons why each head seems to be coming from the other.

—A.J.

11

The New Guard:

Placido Domingo and

Sherrill Milnes

E'S SORT OF A LOVABLE TEDDY BEAR," Sherrill Milnes says of Placido Domingo. "The girls love him and want to hug him. I think I'm less of a teddy bear and more of a jock."

"A what?" Domingo asks.

"A jock. You know, athletic, butch. The all-American football singer."

Baritone Milnes and tenor Domingo are engaged in discussing each other's public image. "I think we are both valuable to the layman's idea of the world of opera," the jock adds. "Our image negates some of the old, bad mystiques of the past."

Sprawled comfortably on a couch in the baritone's rambling New York apartment, the singers hardly look like ranking members of the Age of Aquarius. But with their colorful shirts, youthful good looks and unoperatic abandon, they don't resemble representatives of the Golden Age very much either. Milnes does look like the football player of his mind's eye, or perhaps the lead cowboy in a horse opera. His sweater and tight-fitting jeans show off a brawny physique to good advantage. Domingo is a dark, curly-haired, romantic Latin type, rather given to heft, and his loose trousers do little to disguise an ample middle.

Free as they are of most of the stereotype characteristics of opera performers, the singers have understandably been promoted and publicized by at least one record company in a manner usually reserved for pop artists. But they are, in fact, prime specimens of jet-age operatic superstars. Their fast-moving careers are wholly of today. Although both have been on the international scene only since the late sixties, they are in demand by almost every major opera house in the world. Recording companies, too, seek them out. Initially, they were both exclusive RCA artists. Today, because RCA cannot always match the operatic projects offered by competitors, they—like most of their big-time colleagues—play the game of label-hopping with great facility. Milnes made his first record album in 1967 and has, at the close of 1973, completed twenty-eight recordings for four companies. Domingo began a year later, and has twenty-four disc appearances on six labels under his generous belt.

What is immediately striking about both is the natural beauty of their voices. Domingo possesses an Italianate tenor of ample size, warm sound and ravishing lyrical quality. Milnes has a big, bright baritone with a ringing top and surprising agility. Both are well-trained musicians and display considerable musical intelligence. Their repertories are large and diverse, and both have been known to learn new parts and perform them on a few days' notice.

The critics have been, for the most part, kind. Some fault has been found with their vocalism per se, but what they have really come under fire for is interpretive superficiality and, on occasion, technical rough-and-readiness. But the carpers feel that Domingo particularly, at thirty-three and even Milnes, at thirty-eight, have the time and means to overcome these shortcomings and develop fully into substantial singing actors.

A new facet of their art was unveiled with the release of an RCA record on one side of which Milnes sings and Domingo conducts, and on the flip side of which they reverse the roles. Largely because of the Met and their RCA obligations, the two have been thrown together on so many occasions that a close friendship has developed between them: hence this unusual project, which both are quick to defend as being more than a commercial gimmick.

"Let me tell you something," Domingo says in his Latinized English. "The results I don't know what they are. But I can assure you it's not a gimmick. I wouldn't allow myself, and I'm sure Sherrill wouldn't either, to do something unless we felt prepared."

"We've both conducted before," Milnes adds. "Placido has with more major-league forces than I have, but the skills are the same and the working with the people is the same."

"I consider very difficult the career of a conductor, especially to create something," Domingo continues. "Not to play music in a monotonous way, but to make something with rubato, accelerando, dynamics. I believe that many of the conductors of today trust orchestras and musicians, who are so good, and don't pay attention to any of these details. Believe me, at least I will be honest. I have my own ideas of what I want the orchestra to do, and I will transmit them, and it will be my honest feeling. I know what I want. I might be wrong, but it is not a gimmick."

Conducting, it appears, is something more than a whim for the Spanish-born tenor. "A secret dream of mine, which I suppose is not a secret anymore, is that I want to be a conductor. It's a very deep thing, but let me put it this way. I don't think, despite everything, that conducting is more exciting than singing. Not for me. I love my career, I'm very happy to sing and I hope I can sing twenty years more. The thing is, in case something goes wrong with the voice, and I am prepared and will be able to be a good conductor, it will be an escape for me. I would always have something to do with music."

Milnes feels similarly about a career in music, but does not believe he would ever opt for conducting. It is not surprising that their backgrounds, though remarkably diverse, are both firmly rooted in music. But neither's is a typical operatic story—which explains, perhaps, their contemporary and often unoperatic outlooks.

They were born six years and many miles apart—Milnes on a farm in Downers Grove, Illinois, Domingo in Madrid. While little Sherrill stayed put and led a typical farm boy's existence, getting up early and milking cows, little Placido was learning the ins and outs of show business. At nine, he emigrated to Mexico with his parents, who formed their own zarzuela company there. Domingo's mother, Pepita Embil, is a popular figure still and in Mexico is often referred to as the "Queen of Zarzuela." Milnes' mother, who died in 1969, was something of a star in her own right: she established and conducted a community choir and was both a singer and a pianist.

As youngsters, both baritone and tenor showed great potential. Sherrill studied the piano and violin as well as voice. In high school, he won a state music contest in five separate categories, yet upon entering college signed up as a premed student. Placido was publicly at the keyboard by the time he was eight. In his teens he studied conducting; for a short while his teacher was Igor Markevitch. At sixteen, he made his debut—as a baritone— with the family troupe in a work called *Gigantes y Cabezudos.* He also conducted zarzuelas, played the piano in night clubs, sang in musical comedies, including a local production of *My Fair Lady,* and even tried his hand at bullfighting.

Domingo's bullring ambitions were probably a little shorter-lived than Milnes' medical aspirations. Within a year, the baritone had switched from medicine to music, but had enough native caution to take education courses so that he could always teach. His first professional job was with the Margaret Hillis Choir, which performs regularly with the Chicago Symphony. In 1960, he took the big step and decided to pursue an operatic career. A year later, he made his debut with Rosa Ponselle's Baltimore Civic Opera as Gérard in *Andrea Chénier.*

Domingo sang his first major operatic role, Alfredo in *La Traviata,* that same year. He had been offered a contract with Mexico City's opera company if he would switch from baritone to tenor—a transition the manager of the company suspected was lurking within him—and did so. For Domingo to become the seasoned veteran he is (he has more than seven hundred performances behind him), he had to travel the usual operatic route—overseas. Milnes, on the other hand, broke the old rule about developing a career abroad. He is strictly an American-made product.

Americans, in fact, are more familiar with him than they might realize. He is the fellow who informed them that "you get a lot to like with a Marlboro." He also advised prospective consumers musically that they couldn't go wrong with other products such as Falstaff beer and Kellogg's cornflakes. "I've made more than $20,000 in residuals alone," Milnes says of the commercials. He eventually stopped making them when opera became a full-time occupation.

Today, both Domingo and Milnes are in the front rank of practitioners in their respective voice categories. Oddly, when viewed in the light of operatic legend, there are more good tenors to compete with Domingo than there are baritones to challenge Milnes for his crown. Both are chiefly hailed for their performances in Italian roles, but they frequently venture into other areas, including contemporary music. They are riding high; they also realize they are far from perfect, and are even willing to criticize one another.

"I have one criticism of Sherrill, and I hope he has one for me," Domingo says. "He is almost too worried all the time thinking about extra high notes. For instance, he sings B-flats and A-naturals, which is very exciting for the public to hear from a baritone. But I think that just now, being at the top of the world as a baritone, he should concentrate more on the register from E to G and A-flat. And give a little more color on the E-natural and the F."

Milnes retorts, "Well, I'm very busy and run around a lot, but Placido does it even more. If I jam my schedule, I don't know what the word is for him. Maybe jam *anche di più.* Also he's been working on one area, and it's grown and will probably grow more. That is, the highest high, B and C. There are parts for a tenor that can't be sung if he doesn't have a high C. For Placido, this is still growing."

"It's still a problem for me," Domingo agrees. "There's an explanation. When I sing cold, I can hit the C, even the D-flat. I sing *Puritani* when I'm completely cold at home. But when I am putting everything behind me, I arrive at a note and the throat, it closes. I have to find a technique to be able to do that because I want to sing the bel canto repertoire.

"It doesn't bother me. I'm just sorry that in some operas, like *Trovatore,* I would like to have the high C rather than the B-natural, because it's more brilliant. Or in *Bohème* and *Faust.* But since I don't have it, I transpose. It's okay. If it would bother me that much, I wouldn't sing those three operas."

There isn't a tenor alive who doesn't warm to the subject of high notes—whether he's got them or not. Milnes, with his explosive upper register, is equally fascinated with the subject. One gets the impression that they could discuss high notes far into the night.

MILNES: Composers were unfair to tenors. If you think that the difference between a tenor and a baritone is a minor third, how many B-naturals does a tenor have versus A-flats for a baritone? The point is that composers didn't write the same number of high notes a minor third lower for the baritone as they did for the tenor.

DOMINGO: I have eighteen B-flats in *Aïda*.

MILNES: I don't have a single G, just two G-flats, in *Aïda*.

DOMINGO: I have read some books about bel canto. All the high C's Rossini wrote were to be sung in falsetto. Everything from A-flat up was. Can you imagine singing *"A te, o cara"* [from Bellini's *I Puritani*] today with a falsetto? You'd be laughed off stage.

MILNES: It was a much smaller vocal approach then. The orchestras were not as big.

DOMINGO: And the pitch was about a tone lower.

MILNES: Those two little membranes [vocal cords] have remained the same, but, as houses and orchestra sizes have grown, we've had to make more sound.

DOMINGO: When people talk about the age of bel canto as being the best, the Golden Age, I don't give a damn and I don't believe it, because they had an easy life. Tenors never sang over the G—it was a falsetto. If I don't have to go over the G, I swear to you I can sing 365 days a year.

MILNES: It's interesting. I can sometimes vocalize to a C, and I don't mean falsetto. But the voice gets narrower and narrower. The higher pitch increases the power of the note, but it has to speak somewhere and the sound gets thin. There's a point where it stops being beautiful.

DOMINGO: It happens to me also. The B-natural I can really hit—strong and with volume. The high C, when I hit it, sometimes it gets narrow. That's the reason I'm afraid to do it, because I cannot attack it with all my strength. Then there's the danger of cracking. I vocalize sometimes to E-flat in voice, not falsetto. But it's one thing to do it when vocalizing, another to do it on stage.

What is it about high notes that drives performers to strain themselves and drives audiences to the point of frenzy?

MILNES: There's a physical sensation in singing high notes that's second only to sex.

DOMINGO: That's a fantastic description. I have another one that's not as good. When you go to an opera, you want the music to touch your heart. You are in a romantic mood, but still the high notes are like the Romans bringing the Christians to the lions. That's the excitement, the savage approach.

MILNES: From the audience point of view, there is the danger element—will he make it? And there are people who dig sound per se so much that a high note with no theatrical connection is enough for them.

Both Milnes and Domingo are wary of audience reaction based solely on high notes. They are also aware of the fact that audiences can be undiscriminating.

DOMINGO: I sang *Tosca* in Turin, and they gave me an ovation after singing the B-natural before Scarpia's entrance. That makes me think that if another tenor will stink in the whole rest of the act, but will hold that note, he will get the same reaction at that moment. This doesn't happen with other publics, who judge you for everything. In London, for example, the audience has a fantastic memory. Because sometimes they don't applaud throughout the whole opera, but at the end they remember this *piano,* that high note.

MILNES: The British public is very unusual. And they can throw you off, because you belt a high note, there's a big cadence and nothing greets you but silence.

DOMINGO: On my debut, I didn't have any applause after the two arias in *Tosca.* But at the end, it was an ovation not to believe. Aaaah! They even brought me a laurel what-you-call-it. . . . You know, there's a colleague of mine who has a chronometer to check how long he holds notes and then to check how long the applause goes on.

MILNES: That's insane. I've checked applause, but only on tapes after I'm home.

High notes and applause—the stuff that makes Italian opera unique among art forms. Both artists have had their fair share of demonstrative ovations, but neither feels that the public displays of affection have gone to their heads.

DOMINGO: If there has been any change in Sherrill, it has been an improvement. Since he has been traveling around the world so much, there have been many changes, even in his personality. Friendly he has always been, but his attitudes, they are different.

MILNES: Perhaps, in a sense, Placido has an advantage over American singers. Being born in Spain, brought up in Mexico, doing a lot of early singing in Israel, he has a more international flavor. He gained sophistication—in a good way—much earlier. Amazingly, though, there's been little change in him. Even with the many enormous successes he's had in lots of theaters, he's still a "buddy" kind of guy. That may not sound like star talk. But, you know, you can be a star and still be a nice guy. At one time, that wasn't in. To be a star, you had to have a mystique. No one would ever see you in public, and you'd race from the dressing room quick into your limousine and be whisked away. People like to elevate you a little bit, but they also like to think of you as a real human being. I think Placido has stayed this way.

So ended the meeting of the Mutual Admiration Society, jock and teddy bear in attendance.

12

The Marrieds: Joan Sutherland and Richard Bonynge

"'M JUST A STOLID OLD COW," Joan Sutherland moos with disarming exaggeration. "That's the way I have to be. If I get all excited, I can't sing." There is nothing more startling than an on-the-level prima donna. Miss Sutherland's husband, conductor Richard Bonynge, considers his wife "the strongest person I've ever met." His wife says of her husband, "I guess physically Richard is a little less strong than I am." Quips Richard laughingly, "Anyone would have to be as tough as a horse to be as strong as you!"

It's getting-down-to-basics-time chez Bonygne, which isn't at all difficult considering that both the lady and gentleman of the household are hardly what one would call grand, even though they have every right to be. Miss Sutherland is, of course, one of the great dramatic coloratura sopranos of this or any other century. Bonynge is a conductor for her and others—as well as artistic director of the Vancouver Opera Association. Together they are a historic team.

Much has been said about that team, and a lot of it has been negative. Bonynge has been accused of riding shamelessly on the coattails of his wife, and his wife has been accused of furthering her husband's career by ramming him down the throats of opera impresarios around the world. This is a superficial and inaccurate appraisal of a unique partnership. For better or for worse, Miss Sutherland is at her optimum when her spouse is in the pit. He, rather than being Mr. Sutherland, as he is often dubbed, is the prime force behind the soprano—the power who not only keeps her running, but keeps her running smoothly. A Lon Chaney of myriad faces, Bonynge is Miss Sutherland's musical policeman, musicological sleuth, vocal coach, accompanist, adviser, vocal psychiatrist and morale-booster. It is he who has virtually created and developed the Sutherland we know today.

Rather lackadaisical in his modesty, Bonynge takes little credit for unearthing his wife's phenomenal upper register and vocal agility. "Right from the start," he recalls, "I used to say, why are you singing this, why don't you try that? It was probably a selfish thing; I wanted her to sing the music I liked. In my mind, I could also hear different things from her. But I don't think it was something I set out to do."

While Miss Sutherland is the first to give Bonynge all the credit in the world for what he has done and continues to do for her, the conductor isn't kidding himself about immortality. "Look down through the centuries," he explains, "and you'll see that people remember a great prima donna, not the conductors or stage designers." Nor is he particularly upset or concerned about the present with its vogue to enhance her while detracting from him. "Let's face it," he says bluntly, "I've worked all my life to make her sing well, so why the hell am I going to get into a tizz if she gets more applause than I do? It's the nature of things. Everybody loves a prima donna or a tenor."

The lack of rivalry between the Bonynges no doubt has a lot to do with the durability of their marriage. Wed in 1954, they have actually known one another since 1945, when they met and worked together in their native Australia. Theirs appears to be a happy union. Miss Sutherland apparently enjoys giving the impression that she is devoted to her husband's every whim, and couldn't care less what her more militant sisters think about it. "I don't approve of women's lib, I think it's a lot of rubbish," she exclaims. "In a marriage, someone has to give in." "Besides," Bonynge interjects, "I'm a Libra. No matter what turns up, I

adapt to it." "Yes," his wife laughs knowingly, "as long as you get your own way." "Well, there you are," Bonynge says.

Seated comfortably in the study of an elegant old Brooklyn house, of which they rent the top two floors, the husband and wife are obviously giving a little performance. But there is no questioning the fact that, both as people and musicians, they are of one mind. Perhaps the best way to describe that mind is to say it is uncomplicated and unflustered. Miss Sutherland, whose passion is needlepoint, works on some slipcovers as she talks. Bonynge just sits back and talks, a warm, throaty chuckle punctuating his words.

A similar sort of inner calm radiates from their music-making. While the soprano is capable of igniting an arsenal of vocal fireworks and often does, her bravura is effortless and transmitted without the barest hint of aggression. She does not indulge in the one-woman artillery-barrage kind of showmanship. In this sense, she is as unassuming and natural onstage as she is offstage. One can only conclude that the ease with which she comports herself stems from a solid sense of security and an outlook that is completely realistic and untinseled. She is also neither greedy nor anxious about her career.

"For heaven's sake," Miss Sutherland exclaims, "there's room in the world for all of us. If somebody else can come along and sing *Semiramide,* for example, I'm delighted. Why should I say it's mine? Also, I only sing twice a week, and I will not run back and forth across the Atlantic. Many singers fly in from the Continent and sing the next night. I always get here a few days earlier. I don't know how the others do it! I think it's a lack of discipline. It's crazy, because they're only shortening their careers."

The lady knows of what she speaks. Critics, particularly these days, are virtually in awe of the consistently high standard of Miss Sutherland's performances and of the fact that her voice is showing few, if any, signs of strain or age. This is her payoff for years of saying no, when she really wanted to say yes. "I've always been ruled by the career," she explains. "It was submissive bondage if you like. You can't have it if you don't do it."

Even Bonynge is rather surprised by how well her voice is holding up. "I thought, being so heavy, it would drop a little. But it doesn't seem to be dropping. And yet it's warmer downstairs than it used to be. You know, for a while Joan was singing the F repertory. On good days now, I suppose, she can scream an F, but she's frightened and doesn't sing them anymore. She even avoids the E-naturals if she can. But in the doll's aria in *Tales of Hoffmann,* which she's doing a lot these days, there are seven E-flats alone.

"But if the voice does drop, she sure as hell is not going to sing *Lucia* or *Sonnambula* anymore. There are plenty of roles which climax at D and D-flat. If the voice drops that much, she could have a crack at Lady Macbeth, which people have been asking her to do for years."

Until that time, Miss Sutherland, aside from an odd excursion here and there, will continue concentrating on the repertory for which she has become famous—those singular ladies of Bellini, Donizetti and Rossini, which appear to be written with her voice in mind. The Bonynges jokingly refer to this area as "the Sutherland repertory," while admitting with enormous grins that Maria Callas might also rightfully claim ownership. The grins become even wider when they discuss what they consider the encroachment on their territory by another current prima donna, and Miss Sutherland's only real rival, Beverly Sills.

BONYNGE: I think she has a big Sutherland complex insofar that she sings all her roles.

SUTHERLAND: Everything I've ever sung.

BONYNGE: It's good in the way that it gives more publicity to these operas and to bel canto. And, of course, Miss Sills has a big publicity machine, so it's fine for everybody. We don't lose anything by it.

SUTHERLAND: I've even had a few people come up to me and say that they heard me sing a performance somewhere or other when I hadn't. I'm sorry, I said, I think it must have been Miss Sills. I wonder if the same thing has happened to her?

BONYNGE: I think it would be quite amusing if the Met put on a *Traviata* with both of them in one season. That's good for business. If one wants to put them in the same opera, where both would have good roles, that's all right too. I don't know if she would accept to do it though. On records you can turn the knobs up, you see.

SUTHERLAND: Now, now, now, what are you saying?

BONYNGE: I'm just stating a truth, my dear.

SUTHERLAND: You know, the public loves a rivalry, especially between prima donnas. In the old days there were even more of them. I think there really is no time for it today, though.

BONYNGE: It should be possible to like both of them. I've heard Miss Sills sing things that have given me a great thrill and which I've admired very much. I've also heard her do things that I don't like, but I've also heard Joan do things that I don't like.

SUTHERLAND: Well, my God, she has technical ability that I don't have, like her marvelous pianissimo. Same thing with Caballé. I can't do it.

BONYNGE: Don't say you can't do it.

SUTHERLAND: No, I can do it, but not the way Caballé can.

BONYNGE: They can do it at the drop of a hat.

SUTHERLAND: If I do it, the only thing is that I can't get the voice back again, so I won't. That's true. Remember, I was once going to stand there and *sprech* all the time singing Wagner.

Miss Sutherland is referring to her days at Covent Garden in the fifties when, as a resident singer, she had to be available for almost any soprano role in the repertory, and all for the glorious fee of $30 a week. Between 1952 when she made her debut, and 1959 when a new production of *Lucia di Lammermoor* literally turned her into a star overnight, Miss Sutherland sang a ridiculously varied gallery of roles including Aïda, Amelia in *Un Ballo in Maschera,* Agathe in *Freischütz,* the Woodbird in *Siegfried,* Eva in *Meistersinger,* Pamina, Queen of the Night and the First Lady in *Die Zauberflöte* and Desdemona in *Otello.*

While everyone else seemed convinced that she would eventually develop into a Wagnerian because of the size of her voice, Bonynge steadfastly kept pushing her toward bel canto and its more delicate music. When his, by then, wife sang Clotilde to Maria Callas' Norma at the Garden, Bonynge used the legendary singer as a prime example of a large-voiced soprano who had conquered the complications of coloratura singing to historic effect. Then came the *Lucia,* and his instincts were proven to be dead-center correct. And it was thus that the towering and stalwart Australian lass, who had once been a typist in order to support herself, hit the international trail and became a superstar.

Long before, Bonynge, despite a considerable talent, had given up any hopes of becoming a concert pianist, and was devoting himself full time to furthering his wife's career. In 1962, a bit bored by being in the background, Bonynge made his conducting debut at a concert in Rome, and since then he and his wife have done most of their performing together.

It was in 1961 that Joan Sutherland came to the Metropolitan as Lucia and caused an enormous stir. Bonynge followed four years later in a new production of the same opera, and generally got roasted for his work on the podium. As he gained more conductorial experience, the critics began relenting in their harsh words, although they have yet to welcome him with open arms as a maestro.

The Bonynges have led a reasonable if unexciting and much too infrequent existence at the Met. They believe that the company erred with the prima donna in two areas. First, both the old and new regimes have been extremely conservative in the repertory they have offered her, putting a heavy emphasis on such bread-and-butter works as *Lucia, Traviata, Don Giovanni, Rigoletto* and *The Tales of Hoffmann.* When they strayed a bit from the norm, it was with equally safe operas like *Norma* and *Sonnambula.* "It really would be nice if they just took the plunge and put on something crazy like *Semiramide, Lucrezia Borgia* or *Maria Stuarda,*" Miss Sutherland says politely.

The soprano is less placid when it comes to describing the quality of the new productions she received at the Met. "Oooh," she explodes, "the *Sonnambula* was ghastly!" Bonynge agrees. "We lost interest in it. It was a punishment to go into the pit and look at it. The *Lucia* was a rotten production also." "Dreadful! Terrible!" his wife adds. "Attilio Colonello and Margherita Wallmann together, uch! I'm sorry, but that was Mr. Bing at his worst, ugh!"

The Bonynges find Schuyler Chapin's regime much more congenial than the preceding one. "They are nicer people to talk to," the conductor reports. "Mr. Bing ruled in an ivory tower and didn't want to be approachable." But, despite the opening of channels, there still seems to be something fouling up communications. During 1973–74, the only Sutherland/Bonynge appearances were in a new production of *Tales of Hoffmann*. In '74–75, they will not be at the house at all, and in '75–76 they are scheduled to partake in a new production of *I Puritani,* but considering the Met's crisis status, no one is taking bets on that happening.

The company has come under great fire for failing to engage a number of major artists. The absence of Joan Sutherland from the Met for an entire season is one of the reasons for the consternation. The situation becomes more deplorable when it is understood why she won't be in evidence. Bonynge explains. "There was a slight misunderstanding. I think perhaps because we're very easygoing, they didn't take us seriously for a moment. They asked us what we'd like to do, and we suggested revivals like *Traviata, Faust* and *Don Giovanni,* one or all three. Then, suddenly, they wanted us to do *Hoffmann* again. We did twenty-two, including the tour, in '73–74, and said no. They kept on trying to persuade us, and finally we accepted other work. When I dare say they might have come around to our way of thinking, it was too late. That was all that happened. There was no row, and there are no ill feelings on either side. But we're missing a season, and are sorry about it in a way."

They're not the only ones. The Met needs all the stars it can get, especially the ones who sell tickets like Miss Sutherland. "You'd think that with *Traviata, Faust* and *Giovanni,* they'd be happy because it would guarantee the house selling out," Bonynge says with bewilderment. "You know, what they must be very careful about and realize is that the Metropolitan Opera is *the* Metropolitan Opera. And I'm sorry if I sound snobbish, but it should be a step above the New York City Opera in actual stars and the level of casting. If they cast people at the Met whom you can go and see the next night at the City Opera, who's going to pay the very high prices demanded?"

At this point in their careers, neither of the Bonynges gets particularly unsettled if scheduled plans fall through or if they suddenly find themselves with spare time on their hands. Bonynge is a mad researcher, and would like nothing more than to be able to spend weeks on end unearthing unusual material for his wife or others to sing. Miss Sutherland in her own words is lazy, so no work for her is always enjoyable.

Less work might also give them the chance to spend more time with Adam, their six-foot, three-inch, eighteen-year-old, sports-loving son. As soon as the subject of the lad comes up, his mother is out of the room in a flash, returning moments later proudly bearing the latest photographs of the strapping, floppy-haired young man. From his infancy, the Bonynges made a tough decision about Adam and have stuck to their guns ever since. That is, they were not going to schlepp him around the world, and have him live in dressing rooms and hotels. Home to Adam is the Bonynges' permanent residence, a chalet above the Lake of Geneva in Switzerland, where he has been brought up by a Swiss housekeeper named Ruthli.

"We didn't drag him around and exhibit him as a celebrity's child," Bonynge says. "We went off and left him," his mother adds. "One time we weren't home for his birthday for eight years. I know, it's terrible. But I don't think it's affected him. He's very sweet to both of us. He's always known that he could come to us if he had problems, that if anything was wrong, we were get in touchable with."

"Actually, our relationship is remarkably close, considering we've been so far apart," Bonynge says. "We're a little worried about him at the moment though. He doesn't seem to know what he wants to do. I said, go to the university and improve your languages. He's already got French, Italian and German."

Neither mother nor father would handle the Adam situation any differently, they claim, had they the chance to do it over again. Nor, they say, would they do anything else any differently than it has been done. Miss Sutherland, in her simple, straightforward manner, explains that they are both quite content with their lot. In a rare moment of candor, she also rather shyly defines her own outlook and why so much of what has happened to her has not greatly altered that outlook.

"I think it's basically because of my solid, down-to-earth Scots parentage," the soprano muses. "They always rather accepted what happened. One was glad to be alive, I suppose, glad that one had survived certain crises. If you get down to it, I suppose one had a rather rigid upbringing, a very strict, Victorian, religious upbringing really. And although one may not strictly attend the church anymore—one goes when one feels like it, to special services perhaps—but in the back of one's mind is the peace and calm that is the mark such an upbringing leaves on one. You can't sort of get away from it.

"I think Richard and I have had a rather fortunate family life. We've tried to do the best we can. Although we've been completely divorced from Adam, we've tried to give him a sense of calm in this household. I mean, we've had our differences of opinion. Those people who say that they have lived together and have never had a difference of opinion must be awfully dull. But I think we just sort of accepted things as they came."

And she will accept them as they come. That includes retirement, of which Miss Sutherland is anything but fearful. "I think about it constantly," she says smiling. "But nobody takes me seriously. They tell me I'd be bored. But I've already done more than I ever expected to, and I don't say that in a boastful way. Why in heavens should I fear retirement? I have a home I would willingly live in. I could cook and garden. You know, I've never really had the chance to be Mrs. Bonynge."

13

The Marrieds:

Marilyn Horne and

Henry Lewis

ARILYN HORNE AND HENRY LEWIS call themselves star-crossed lovers, which may be romanticizing it a bit, but there is no denying that, as a couple, the Lewises have signed up for a lifelong roller-coaster ride. While such excursions are often entertaining, the element of constant surprise can become enervating. Statistics tell us that show business marriages are pretty much doomed anyway. Add an integrated ingredient and the chances for survival become infinitesimal. But, wed since 1960, the Lewises no doubt will survive. Time has taught them that the fact she is white and a singer and he is black and a conductor has been the least of their problems. What vex the couple are the conflicts that arise when two potent, aggressive and highly individualistic personalities clash—head on and often.

"If you'll pardon the allusion," Lewis explains, laughing heartily, "we are like salt and pepper." Indeed, even in their physical appearances, they are opposites. Miss Horne is an always ticking, smallish time bomb—squat, plump and cuddly—with an infectious throaty roar and an unaffected sense of humor one rarely sees onstage. Lewis is externally more serene—tall, well-built and striking—with an air of arrogance that disappears once he is relaxed, and an outlook seemingly complex and serious. Until he is at ease, one also gets the impression he is trying to prove something.

"We care enough to fight about things," the husband says. "That's true," his wife adds. 'We are not giver-uppers in the face of problems. Our marriage has been fraught with all the usual anxieties, plus a thousand more." "You may not want me to say this, but we've also had help," Lewis continues. "We've both been under some kind of psychiatric care—not joint—for a while, and its helped us immensely to grow. Actually, I'm sort of proud of it."

Comfortable in the cluttered music room of their big and beautiful East Orange, New Jersey, home, the Lewises continue discussing the various facets of an eventful marriage when the lady of the house unwittingly drops a clinker.

HORNE: Let's face it, the most important thing with us is that there has been a deep love, and *never* any hint of a third person or any kind of outside involvement. That shows a lot of trust and security, doesn't it, Henry?

LEWIS: Hints there have been.

HORNE: [Shrieks with laughter.]

LEWIS: Remember?

HORNE: No, Henry.

LEWIS: I've heard a *hint* or two from you, haven't I?

HORNE: All right, that just keeps it spicy.

LEWIS: That's quite all right with me. Trust is fine, but we shouldn't be so dull between ourselves that we take each other for granted. A few weeks ago I went to Chattanooga with our daughter Angela to visit some friends while Jackie [Miss Horne's nickname] went to California to do the Tonight Show and *The Odd Couple*. She didn't call for four days, and I was fit to be tied. My friends said, 'Oh, you know she's just visiting her family.' I said, I don't know any such thing! I haven't heard from her in four days.

HORNE: Poor Jackie was working ten hours a day at the studio. I had a terrible cold, and I'd come back to the hotel and just fall into bed.

LEWIS: That's just fine. I put a little mystery into things, and you just take it right out! Anyway, smooth and glassy seas it has not been. But it's alive.

Of late, Mr. and Mrs. Lewis have been going their separate

ways professionally. For a period, they seemed to be doing everything together. There was even a time when it seemed that music director Lewis couldn't bring his New Jersey Symphony across the Hudson without the presence of den mother Horne. Rumors started spreading that the conductor was afraid to play a New York stand without the box office and musical support of his wife. Eventually they were advised by their manager and friends that it was not good for either of their careers to perform together so often.

"That was because of what people supposedly think, which always bugs me," Lewis exclaims. "My orientation has always been to do the music I like with the people I like. True success comes from quality, not from planning something which is supposed to create the impression. I must say though that the New Jersey Symphony had a very successful series of concerts during the 1973–74 season without Marilyn—and it was calculated that she shouldn't be with us. It seemed we weren't able to use her for even one out of three concerts without people writing reams about how we were resting on Marilyn's laurels.

"As a result of this, the orchestra, for the first time, was really exposed. Somehow, through odd programming or one thing or another, I had kept the orchestra from being absolutely on the line. But with the particular pieces I had chosen this time, there was no way out. This had a great effect. People suddenly were reading much more about me and the New Jersey Symphony without it being Marilyn. It's helped the general attitude because she's also doing more opera and things with other people.

"The best thing about it is that we've reached the point now where people are beginning to say, would you two do something together? And they ask this without feeling that they *have* to take me with Marilyn à la other couples."

Lewis is alluding, of course, to Joan Sutherland and her husband, Richard Bonynge. The Lewis/Bonynge parallel was established years ago when their two wives worked together with great frequency. Today they are still teamed up, but much less often. Under any circumstances, the comparison is unjust. While Bonynge is, first and foremost, his wife's accompanist, Lewis is a conductor with his own orchestra. He is interested and involved in a much broader scope of music-making. Also, Miss Sutherland will usually not partake in a project unless her husband is leading the band, whereas Miss Horne has and does perform with various maestros. People talked, however, and for a time Henry Lewis was known in some circles as Mr. Horne.

He is aware of this, makes no effort to deny it and will openly discuss it. "It wasn't a problem for us because neither of us believed it. Sometimes people would say something to me or to her, and she would get angry and defend me. Once we had an enormous fight and I said, 'Don't you *dare* defend me because there's nothing to defend!'

"I honestly never thought there was. I knew what I was responsible for and how we started. I knew that for years I was the sole breadwinner. And even then I knew that if she became successful, she would eventually make more money than I could hope to make at the peak of my career, because she was a singer, a diva.

"What occasionally does bother me is that the life of a prima donna is difficult. Unless we're very careful—and this is something we're working on now—the illusion comes about that Jackie is willing to or does put herself out a great deal for things concerning Marilyn Horne. She must dress up, go out and simulate a certain kind of ambience. But then she should be able to come home, relax and not have to bother with these things. Sometimes there is a problem about the idea of Marilyn Horne as opposed to Mrs. Lewis, and having the energy for one and not the other. That's the only area where her career becomes something of a source of jealousy for me. I'm sometimes jealous of the energy it takes away from being Mrs. Lewis."

Mrs. Lewis agrees. "There are a lot of things concerning the home that I don't have the energy for because of all the energy that has to go into the career. In this day and age, it is very difficult to find the people to do them for you." The mezzo stops and thinks for a moment. "You know," she continues, "I might have put Henry in the position of being Mr. Horne many times because I *want* him to conduct for me. Henry conducting the operas he has taught and prepared me for is the greatest thing I can have."

The couple met when she was a voice student at the University of Southern California and he was a bass player with the Los Angeles Philharmonic. Miss Horne is a native of Bradford, Pennsylvania, but moved to the West Coast with her family in 1945, when she was eleven. Lewis, who is two years older than his wife, was born in Los Angeles. Ever since their marriage in 1960, which was met with great familial resistance, later overcome, the conductor has taken over the singer's musical stewardship. Other than his constant overseeing of her vocal resources—something no singer should be without—Lewis is solely responsible for Miss Horne's being the unique kind of singer she is today: a bel canto specialist with an extended freak range that defies the normal boundaries associated with the soprano or mezzo-soprano voice. It is because of this extension in her voice that Miss Horne is also able to venture into repertories far afield from Bellini, Donizetti and Rossini.

"We have no illusions that without Henry I wouldn't have had a career," Miss Horne says. "But I must say that the difference in my career, the quality of it, has been Henry. For instance, he labored and sweated and did everything he could to teach me the style of the kind of music I have become famous for. And he's written all those damn cadenzas, arpeggios and two-octave drops. I had never done a bel canto opera until the *Beatrice di Tenda* in New York in 1961. Henry had been immersed in this music since he was a teen-ager. The style was so foreign to me, I can remember taking the score and throwing it across the room screaming, 'I hate this music!'"

"What she actually said," Lewis interjects, "was that it was a pile of crap and who needs it?" The conductor credits a facet of his own makeup for envisioning that his wife should sing the music in the first place, and then forcing her to stick with it. "I have a practical side. I think I saw a hole in the firmament of stars in the world and I said, Jackie, if you want to fit into it, you've got to find an empty spot, otherwise you won't get in. Even though you don't like this bel canto stuff, at the moment I can see a place for the kind of success you want if you will capitalize on that in order to get your position. Then you can do what you want from that realm of authority. The gift was already there, but not the extension that she's famous for. We labored for that— every single note. You can count a year per half step."

Miss Horne's memories of that trying period are equally vivid, particularly the discouragement she felt watching singers move ahead who had not been at the game nearly as long as she had. In an effort to increase her experience, she had even gone to Europe. There, between 1956 and 1960, she had gotten her feet wet with a diverse repertory, including such soprano parts as Mimì in *La Bohème,* Minnie in *Fanciulla del West,* Tatiana in *Eugene Onegin* and Amelia in *Simon Boccanegra.*

"Whenever I'd complain, Henry used to say to me, listen, so-and-so is like a shot glass that's flowing over. You are a tumbler that's only half full and people hear you struggling for that other half, because there's so much more to get. Henry's always the leader in our relationship in innovative things. I am terribly cautious, in spite of the fact that I am probably the loudmouth of the two of us."

Lewis smiles in agreement, and then says seriously, "Jackie's incredible talent is to accept information like a computer. In goes all my research, and in the manner of a truly 'touched' person, it comes out something else and all put together."

It's a two-way street for the Lewises. While, in a strict sense, he has "taught" her, she, in a more subtle fashion, has aided him considerably in his conducting. A colorist, Lewis is deeply concerned with the physical sound of his orchestra. A great deal of his sensitivity in this important aspect of music-making has come from listening to his wife. "I think I have been affected by Jackie's incredible sound and by our working on how to make it uniform," he explains. "She has the ability to color her sound and, for example, to lighten it while still retaining its substance.

"If there is anything I would personally pat myself on the back for, it is creating the sound of the New Jersey Symphony, of making a real sound out of nothing. That is because I consciously went after it, and in rehearsals would say, everything is fine, except it's the wrong kind of sound. Let's color it this way. For years, I had to make them overplay. They didn't have the concept of a big enough sound. Now I often have to pull them back, because when they play you sense this enormous reserve which they never ever touch, even at their loudest."

Not bashful, Miss Horne would often advise her husband in these matters. "I remember I used to tell him that I couldn't hear the first flute player, that he should fire her. But he had this vision, and would answer that a beautiful and sweet tone was really there. He was right, and it took him two or three years to get it out. Now it's wonderful.

"Once Lennie Bernstein said to me that he couldn't under-

stand why Henry wasn't just traveling all over the world conducting every orchestra. I told Lennie that maybe Henry's doing
what he wants to do. He's really from the old tradition. There
were hardly any guest conductors fifty years ago."

Lewis nods in agreement. "People often say to me, how can
you stand it, conducting all the concerts and rehearsals. But that's
my interest. One of the reasons the orchestra has been so effective
up to now is because they are concentrating on one person's
ideas." Lewis believes that today's jet-age maestros are a new
breed of musicians whose outlook is alien to him. "I sense something missing," he says. "They are coming up too quickly. Personal magnetism or something pushes them forward in their
twenties when they have no experience. The older I get, the
more convinced I am that conducting is an old man's business,
not because you have to be old, but because there's so much to
know. Orchestras want to choose conductors and programs and
run everything almost entirely by themselves. This kind of attitude adds to their desire for the kind of conductor who does
not want to change things and does not want to create a sound."

The Lewises could both afford the luxury of building their
careers slowly on the basis of long-term planning because at no
point since their marriage has either of them had to go and "get
a job." Financial stability gave them the patience and stamina
to say no to those offers which, though initially pleasing or
lucrative, might have been out of kilter with what they foresaw
for themselves. As Lewis aptly points out, "This is the way
Jackie was able to make herself a star mezzo-soprano."

By some peculiar quirk of operatic madness, sopranos and
tenors can much more easily ascend to superstardom than their
lower-voiced equivalents, mezzos and baritones. Thanks to her
vocal and musical abilities, and clever and careful management,
Miss Horne has become something of a superstar mezzo—surely
the first one at the Metropolitan since Risë Stevens.

This has been no mean feat because, according to the lady
herself, the Met has not begun to even scratch the surface of the
repertory she has sung or is willing to sing. Now that Lewis
has conducted at the house as well—the first black maestro with
the company, he made his debut in 1972 leading *La Bohème,*
and then took over for Leonard Bernstein in the *Carmen* produc-

tion—the couple has much to say on the subject of the Metropolitan.

HORNE: Although I have had three terrific productions at the Met, *Norma, Carmen* and *L'Italiana in Algeri,* I have a scope that has not been touched in New York, and which could and should be expanded. I think I'm a valuable enough singer —at the box office, too. How about all the bel canto operas I would like to sing? And aren't we due for a whopping Meyerbeer opera? Somebody from the management once said to me, I understand you want to sing *Semiramide* at the Met. I said, look, all I know is that the most successful team to come to the Met since God-knows-who is Joan Sutherland and me. Now, the fact that the Met didn't immediately engage us for another opera after *Norma* back in 1970 is a total mystery to me. It's unbelievable, in fact. *Semiramide* is an opera we have on the books and could pull out in just a couple of weeks. If not that, how about Bellini's *Capuletti,* which is one of his greatest operas.

LEWIS: Let me interrupt. *Semiramide* and *Capuletti* are the ones they should really do for Jackie. She has developed the ability to do the young hero (trouser part) in the style of Pasta and Malibran, of singing these roles in the grand manner in which they were written. Put her and Joan Sutherland into one of these things, and you'll really get a taste of what it was like in those days. As for Meyerbeer, the only viable opera is *Prophète. Huguenots* is awfully tricky, because you really have to have five great singers. *Prophète* takes three singers, chorus and staging.

HORNE: The other thing is, I would like to do some of the Verdi parts now. Bing did ask me to sing Eboli in *Don Carlo,* but I can't jump in without any rehearsals. It has to be planned. Also, I really want to test my wings in some of the Wagner and German repertory.

LEWIS: She has a feeling in her bones she could be a great *Fidelio* Leonore. She really wants to sing that. You know, all this talk keeps reminding me of the Edward Johnson era. Look at the development that went on then, how he managed American singers like Eleanor Steber, Richard Tucker, Robert Merrill, Risë Stevens, Roberta Peters and Jan Peerce. Most of these people he planned for and helped are still singing today. Part of the job of an opera house is to build their gifted singers.

As Marilyn Horne and Henry Lewis discuss artistic matters, whether their own, the Met's or the New Jersey Symphony's, it soon becomes clear that they both set enormously high standards for themselves and others. But, like so many other aspects of their existence, they are disparate here too, not about what they want, but the way to go about getting it. Miss Horne best describes the difference.

"I hate the word *perfectionist,* it turns my stomach," she says. "But Henry has this drive to make everything as perfect as possible. I do not. He pushes me sometimes to extend myself, despite a great force working against him from my corner. I have to thank him for that."

Today, Lewis understands this about himself. Once he didn't. "I have learned that when I let things go, it doesn't always mean disaster. We're already working on a pretty high level. True, I can see another world, but what we're doing is valuable and I shouldn't stand there all night trying to make it better."

In many ways, Lewis the perfectionist, the idealist, is more realistic than Miss Horne. He is obviously a man who gives much thought to a subject, and is probably even a brooder. As she herself admits, Mrs. Lewis is the "loudmouth" of the family, and sometimes tends to react emotionally to a subject, whereas her husband will retain more objectivity. This contrast in their personalities comes to light particularly when they talk about Angela, their friendly, intelligent and lovely-looking daughter.

HORNE: Angela is number one. She comes above everything.

LEWIS: That isn't quite accurate.

HORNE: Henry, I disagree with you.

LEWIS: That's the difference between you and me.

HORNE: We consider Angela and her welfare practically above everything else. She knows that if she has a cold and is sick in bed and somebody has to take care of her, if we have a performance, we've got to go, but she knows she will be well taken care of in that respect.

LEWIS: You see what you're saying. You want it one way, but it really isn't. That's "magical" thinking—the way you would like it to be. She's our daughter, wonderful, and it should sound like that. But it *isn't* like that. She is our daughter and I love her, and if I was required to have my legs cut off in order to save her from having hers cut off, my legs would be cut off. In that sense, she's number one. But there is something false in someone else being number one. You are first yourself. Angela's got to be an individual. I love her as much as I've ever loved anybody in terms of cherishing, but she will leave us in seven years. I think she's secure. Experts, child psychologists say so too. I can only hope. One thing I do know. We have tried very hard to make her feel loved, and to make her feel that nothing in particular is required of her.

HORNE: Back to me saying she's number one. If it were ever push to shove, Angela would come first. If it were down the line required, I'd give up my career. I'd do it for Henry, too.

LEWIS: If somebody said that Angela will, like Sleeping Beauty, wither and die if you don't stop singing, of course you would. But, if she said, "Mommy, I don't want you to sing anymore," you wouldn't stop, would you?

HORNE: No. She's very bright and early on, when she was one and two, she would start to scream and cry whenever I sang. When she finally began to talk, as soon as I would start to practice, she would start to cry and say, "Mommy can't sing anything." I said, I know a lot of people who would agree with you.

LEWIS: There's one fear I have. Angela's seen herself be sick, Jackie be sick, me be sick. And yet, if there's a concert we go. Other things are put off, but not concerts. I think she knows that. It may be that we've done well, and as she grows up, she will understand. I hope that's the way it is. But in her mind, I think she is a little bit sorry she isn't absolutely first.

HORNE: Angela, more with me than with Henry, has said she would just as soon that I didn't sing. But I've got a joke on her. She's got a terrific voice, and she may be a singer herself. Ask her now if she wants to be one, and she'll say no. But she's got a terrific voice.

14

Up from the Ranks:
Mignon Dunn

IGNON DUNN FINALLY DID IT—got herself an opening night and mopped up. It was like the return of the native at the Met's 1973 opening when the lusty mezzo from Memphis burned up the stage as Azucena, demented gypsy lady of Verdi's *Il Trovatore,* walked away with an armload of critical paeans and at long last came into her own as an artist to be reckoned with—fifteen years and forty-five roles after coming to the Metropolitan.

Success agrees with her. "I've been in such revolting good humor that it's just nauseating," Miss Dunn announces in a deep-throated Southern belle drawl. "I don't know how Lee Marvin felt after he won the Academy Award for *Cat Ballou,* but *I* felt incredible. Frankly, I wasn't even conscious for the first half page of music. I can't remember ever being so nervous in my whole life. A great deal was riding on it for me. You can sing all over the world at the finest houses, but when you come back home, the Met is still *the* big one."

So is Miss Dunn. She may measure in at a mere five feet nine inches, but in the flesh—of which there's a womanly plenitude— she is Amazonian, fearless in huge high heels, bouffant brunette hair, and a blue and white polka dot pants suit which, as she sashays about, clings shamelessly to her ample contours. "I don't know if I come on strong or not," she muses, "but I look taller than I am. I'm not exactly skinny either, nor am I big-boned. I'm just fat."

She carries her endowment gracefully. There were days when she stalked about onstage with bended knees, especially when her leading men were Lilliputians. Then the late Tyrone Guthrie, directing her in an opera, asked rather pointedly, "You cow, what on earth are you doing?" That settled that. Now she's all legs, and they're as straight as the columns on Blue Briar, the super-Southern mansion in which Miss Dunn spent her early childhood.

In New York, she has had to adjust to an airy West Side studio apartment, leased late in 1973. Decorating it is taking a long time because she is traveling so much, and making one successful debut after another in a number of European capitals. But at least she can finally settle down in New York because she finally has a Met career worth—for sure—the price of an apartment.

The mezzo, who refuses to disclose her age ("I've been singin' so long, people think I'm a lot older than I am"), is at a turning point in her career. For the first time, she appears to have a chance really to hit the international big time. What has kept her on the outskirts all these years is a mixture of personal and circumstantial situations, none of which she particularly relishes talking about.

"I have a tendency not to dwell on unpleasant things," she says seriously. "A lot of singers are late bloomers. Giulietta Simionato was. I certainly think that, of course, it could have come earlier. But I'm glad it's coming now. Possibly I'm more equipped to handle it now. Who knows? Maybe I'm rationalizing because I don't want to feel too bad about those times."

Those times were at the Metropolitan in the sixties when Miss Dunn, naïve and craving work, bound herself to seasonal contracts which forced her to hang around covering almost everything (her first year with the company she learned *every* mezzo and contralto part in the Ring), while only occasionally getting a scrap here or a cookie there. She even managed to build up an impressive sheaf of reviews, none of which seemed to be read by the powers at the house. As early as 1961, Harold C. Schonberg predicted that she had the "makings of a great Amneris." Four years later, she proved she was a great Dalila, but to no avail.

"I really don't want to dwell on the old regime—it's over and finished with," the singer says, carefully trying to offend no one. "But I'll give you one hint of the way things worked, and that's all. I don't know quite how to say this, but when you got to a certain plateau, there was no way they'd let you go past it.

"I did the Dalila, and later that same week I was called in to talk about the contract for next year. Mr. Bing said he had a marvelous new production for me. He wanted me to do the Second Lady in *The Magic Flute*. With that I knew it was *basta, finito*. I just laughed and said no."

Even prior to this incident, Miss Dunn had had enough sense to take off for Germany, where she landed a contract with the Düsseldorf Opera. It was in Düsseldorf and then Hamburg and other European cities that the mezzo had the chance not only to sing lead parts in new productions, but to refine her art and learn to command the stage with the authority she radiated as Azucena.

In the 1971–72 season, when she returned to the Met to sing Brangäne in the new *Tristan,* Miss Dunn in essence paved the way for her recent opening night and the exciting years she has ahead of her. Ironically, it is only now that she is being allowed to repay the trust the Met had in her long ago when its talent scouts heard her as a seventeen-year-old in Memphis, encouraged her to come to New York and eventually gave her a scholarship.

The financial aid supported her lessons (for many years with Karin Branzell) but was not enough to support her. To make a living, Mignon Dunn became Marianne Grey, nightclub singer, who was heard in Yorkville haunts, the Latin Quarter, the Borscht Belt and Las Vegas (with Milton Berle). Whether as Miss Grey or Miss Dunn, the singer was able to find work—in the chorus of *The Saint of Bleecker Street,* as a leading lady of the Amato Opera Company and finally as Carmen with the New York City Opera in 1956. After a short period with the City Opera, Miss Dunn was grabbed by the Met, where she made her debut as the Nurse in *Boris Godunov* on October 29, 1958.

Throughout this period and the frustrating years that followed, the mezzo always put her work first, "but I never did the outside things—like going places you're supposed to go, and being nice to people you're supposed to be nice to. It would never have come off anyway. If I don't like a person it shows. I'm simple and not devious. I suppose I never really thought in terms of a 'career.'"

Does she now? Is superstardom what she is striving for? "I want to do the roles I want to do, in theaters where I can do them well. If you gotta be a superstar to do that, fine. But to be a superstar per se, no. I wouldn't want to ever think I was losing face just because I was doing Anna in *The Trojans*. There are great parts that are also not star parts."

Even some of the biggest mezzo parts are second-banana roles. That doesn't ruffle Miss Dunn either. "I'm happy being a mezzo," she exclaims. "Good lord, these are the acting parts, the meat. What could be better than Carmen, Amneris, Azucena? I wouldn't swap 'em for a soprano part for anything. The only role I think should have been written as a mezzo—and believe me I'm never going to do it—is Tosca. She has a mezzo personality. It was mean of Puccini not to write that down a little bit."

Miss Dunn's taste runs to the more melodramatic works. "I'm just not a Mozart singer. I choke to death. Actually, I would adore to sing Dorabella, but I don't think I could get hired. People think of me in more dramatic parts. I'm really burning to do different things like *La Favorita, Le Prophète,* and *Hérodiade.*"

She would like to record too, and reports that since her New York and European triumphs, there have been feelers from various companies. She would also like to do more orchestra concerts and recitals, areas in which she can get a lot of help at home.

In 1972, the singer married Kurt Klippstaetter, director of the Memphis Opera and Arkansas Orchestra. It was the second marriage for both. Initially, when they met in the sixties in Düsseldorf, where Klippstaetter was a conductor/coach, the relationship was purely professional until the day the mezzo "fell like a thunderbolt. I couldn't believe it; I was the most shocked soul in the world."

The Klippstaetters have three residences—a new home in Little Rock, a small residence in Memphis and the apartment in New York. Although their individual careers keep them apart, "whenever we have two days free, we're always together." That Miss Dunn is, for the nonce, more successful than her husband poses no strain on their happiness. "Kurt's secure enough to handle it. He would be very upset with me if I did not do as well as I could. There is no jealousy. In fact, he pushes me into doing more things. In 1974, for the first time, we're going to work together doing the Mahler Wayfarer Songs, which he taught me.

"I hope things keep going the way they are now, both personally and in my career. I also hope Kurt has the success he deserves. He's an incredible musician and has an incredible brain. He also loves America. We understand each other's dedication to our work. We don't cancel performances or rehearsals just to be together longer. We have an enormous phone bill instead."

Miss Dunn stops and thinks for a moment. "If I'm comin' off as Miss Goody Two Shoes, I sure don't mean it, 'cause I'm not. But I'm very happy these days. There was a bad time to go through, but that's over. I have to appreciate what I have now—and I do."

15

A Rebel of Sorts:

Renata Scotto

RENATA SCOTTO HAS AN AMUSING HABIT of prefacing something wicked she is about to say with a very girlish, giggly and Italianate, "Oh, I want not to be naughty." Confession completed, she poises herself and strikes. The soprano's aim is well-nigh perfect. Her target is the Metropolitan Opera where she vows, she will sing no more unless . . .

"I sing for eight years at the Met," Miss Scotto exclaims, "and I don't have one new production, never, and no opening night either! I will not sing at the Met again until they give me a new production or opening night of some interesting opera for me and for the audience. They offer me *Butterfly. I don't want to sing* Butterfly! I know the public. They like me and want me in something different, something new.

"You know, La Scala has for me ten new productions and two opening nights. This is true of other companies too, but I talk about La Scala because it is equal to the Met. All the Met say to me is compliments—*brava, stupenda, meravigliosa,* great success. Then they offer me *Butterfly.* Maybe with the new management something will be changed. I can't say that it is better than the old one, because they don't ask me nothing and nobody talk with me about my future."

Scotto is not unlike the typical Italian prima donna. She expects the world at her feet, but is in no way haughty about the request. It's coming to her. As she sits on the sofa in her Central Park South hotel suite, hands tucked snugly under her thighs, knees clamped together, she is intelligent, charming and, in her own words, *dolce* (sweet). *Dolcezza* notwithstanding, one would hardly want to tangle with her.

Scotto has made a specialty of singing Donizetti, Bellini and Verdi. She does not believe in voice categories such as coloratura, lyric and spinto, and dubs herself simply a soprano, thereby including in her repertory a wide range of parts. To the lighter roles she has for the most part been singing, she soon plans to add Norma, Anna Bolena, the Amelias in both *Un Ballo in Maschera,* and *Simon Boccanegra,* and possibly *Aïda*—all women of a heftier persuasion.

Like most red-blooded Italian ladies who sing for a living, Scotto has a well-ordered sense of logic that does not encompass divergent points of view—particularly about her vocal art. To her way of thinking, there are currently no other sopranos who do justice to the repertory she sings. *Her* way is *the* way.

Heaven forbid someone like a conductor should come along and announce that *his* way is *the* way. "In opera, the singer comes before everything," she says flatly. "The prima donna is prima. The conductor must be a good accompanist, but the singer must be first. Many times I have had discussions, sometimes fights, and always I win. Last year in Italy I was singing *Traviata* and I had a conductor—aaah, terrible! He don't understand me, and he don't want to accompany me. At a rehearsal, he want one tempo and he say, 'You must come with me.' I scream, 'No, maestro, *you* must come with *me*!' Then I stop the rehearsal and go to my dressing room. He follow and I scream, *'I don't want to sing with you anymore!* You don't understand what I feel!' In the performance, he followed me, but with no communication, by force. It was the first and last time I sing with that conductor."

In Italy, where Scotto is something of a national heroine, she can get away with rejecting or accepting a conductor or a fellow singer. In a sense, the cavalier attitude upholds a tradition among tempestuous prima donnas. "I prefer choosing my partner," she says with specific reference to tenors. The tenors she prefers choosing are Nicolai Gedda and Giuseppe di Stefano—"when he sang." As for conductors, she dislikes, among others, Georges Prêtre who "doesn't understand singers. He just thinks about himself. Francesco Molinari-Pradelli is difficult, too. But with me there are not too many troubles. I know very well what I want. I'm reasonable. I like Gianandrea Gavazzeni, Claudio Abbado, Carlo Felice Cillario, Herbert von Karajan and many others."

Scotto's grit burgeoned from a spirit that revealed itself in her youth. Born in Savona, on the northwest Ligurian coast of Italy, Renata was something of an adorable terror. "I think I'm born to sing," she says, her face lighting up with a wondrous smile. "I don't even remember when I started. I was too little. When I was four, my mother told me I used to go out on the terrace of our house and sing. The neighbors gave me candy. I sing all my life. I remember, too, I used to put on my mother's clothes and go to the mirror and perform. I was a difficult child —nice but difficult. Every moment I wanted to be a star, a prima donna, and I'd go to my mother and say, 'Mama, you like this? Mama, *look* at me!' I would sing and perform and my mother said, 'Enough already. Basta!' This happened all the time."

Like so many Italian children, Renata did her share of singing in church choirs. Her ambitions were not operatic until she heard a performance of *Rigoletto* with Tito Gobbi. Then, at twelve, she tried to audition, but was told she was rushing things. Despite this, within a few years she was performing in public— as a mezzo-soprano. At sixteen, she moved to Milan and began serious vocal studies with the great Spanish singer, Mercedes Llopart, who effected the change from mezzo to soprano.

In 1953, the young singer won an Italian competition which set up her formal debut, as Violetta in *La Traviata,* at the Young Artists' Theater in Milan. Within a year, she was invited to La Scala as Walter (a pants part) in *La Wally,* opposite Tebaldi and Del Monaco. The next year she purposely accepted another lesser part, Sophie in *Werther,* at the Rome Opera. Slowly, she began the process of establishing herself.

When La Scala asked Scotto to join them at the Edinburgh Festival in 1957, she was still something of an unknown commodity. But when she stepped in—on three days' notice—for Maria Callas in *La Sonnambula,* her big-time career began in earnest and has continued since.

Although many great divas have triumphed as replacements, Scotto does not believe that hers is a typical case. She feels that her success has to do with the spirit of Maria Malibran (1808–

36), a Paris-born singer who combined a natural contralto with a soprano range. Scotto claims she dislikes talking about the subject, but manages to bring it up herself. "I am very, very close to Malibran," she relates hesitantly. "When I was a student in Milano, I had a friend who invited me to a meeting—aah, is very difficult to explain about mediums.

"I was eighteen, and didn't understand nothing about these things. In this meeting, they said that Malibran wants to talk with me. She said, you will sing my operas—*La Sonnambula, I Capuletti ed i Montecchi*. I didn't believe it. That was in 1953. In 1957, I was asked to replace Callas in *Sonnambula*. I didn't know the part. I don't know what happened, but in three days I learned it and sang it with the most success. I was very sure of me, and I don't know why. It was the most beautiful evening in my career. Now I believe in Malibran. I believe, but I don't want to talk about it."

The spirit of Callas, like Malibran's, also seems to haunt Scotto. Aside from the 1957 incident, she is frequently compared to the legendary singer—which irks her ("I want to be Scotto"). Yet Callas is one of the few retired singers of this generation of whom Scotto speaks with admiration. This didn't stop her, however, from going to the Italian press and brewing up a rip-snorting *scandalo* when the Callas cult attended her 1970 La Scala opening and behaved in a manner which incensed her.

"The Callas fanatics came to my first *Vespri Siciliani* because Callas was in the theater, and they applauded her. They applauded her when I'm the singer. I was furious, and I wrote in all the newspapers and magazines against these fanatics. In the next performance, these people were against me. They came and booed me because I said, 'Callas, if you want to sing, please come to me and I'll let you sing, *if you can!*' I said, you fanatics are against art, against music. *I* am the one who is singing *Vespri*, not La Callas. It's fine to have respect for her, but she *was*. She is past. Now you have to go with me, not against me. Oh, did I write!"

It is curious that this mild-mannered and seemingly docile woman is capable of the fits of wrath she relates fast and furiously. Perhaps because she appears to segregate her career from her private life, she really means it when she says, "On the stage, I want to keep my audience, to interest them. Not off the stage.

Then I am Renata Scotto, woman, private." Even her numerous fans, who she feels are important for her career, are kept at a distance when they try to infringe on her family's time.

"The fans try to call me," she says. "They try once, twice, but no more because they know I don't want to be disturbed. I am very detached. I accept the compliments, I thank them, but they understand. Backstage is something else. I want them in my dressing room, and at the Met I put their names on the list so they can come."

Scotto is protective of her time with her children—Laura and Filippo—because she is rarely with them for concentrated periods. She is married to Lorenzo Anselmi, a former concertmaster of the La Scala orchestra, who left his post to devote his time to his family and to act as his wife's teacher and coach. The soprano realizes it is difficult to be the husband of a prima donna, but claims Anselmi is too intelligent to be bothered by the title Mr. Scotto.

She has yet to come to grips with the problems of having a career and being a mother. She doesn't, for example, take her children with her when she tours. "For my egotism, I sacrifice my children to travel? No! What's going to happen when they get older, I don't know. When they are six, seven, they have to go to school, and they need their parents near. It's a big problem.

"Even now it's a problem. I remember my girl say the night before I left for here, 'Mama, why you sing? Why?' I don't answer because I don't know what to answer. Finally, I say, 'I sing because mama have to sing.' 'But, mama,' she say, 'if you sing, who will wake me in the morning?' Oh. Oh. You don't know me. When I speak of my child, I cry."

Renata Scotto sat there and cried.

16

A Met Star at Last: Shirley Verrett

MALL WONDER SHIRLEY VERRETT is fond of saying her *real* Metropolitan Opera debut occurred in October 1973—when she blew everybody's mind by singing a historic marathon performance of both Cassandra and Dido in *The Trojans*. It wasn't until then that she really made it big in this town, although she had formally come to the house in 1968. Actually, the black mezzo first hit the long, rocky road to the Met in 1961 when she was invited by the Bing administration to sing less than stellar contralto parts in the Wagner operas. Furious with what she considered the insulting idiocy of the offer, Miss Verrett flatly turned them down.

"I am *not* a contralto!" she snaps, hot under the collar just thinking about the incident. "I learned then that most opera house managements just don't care. If you're stupid enough to listen to them, then go on, dear, just ruin that voice. Also, when I entered the Met, I wanted to go straight through the front door, and this has nothing to do with color or anything. This has to do with my personality and how I like to do things."

How she likes to do things is with panache, as a star turn, and that's why the stubborn and often hotheaded singer turned down a second offer from the House of Bing—again because she considered it unsuited to her talents. Warned, however, that three strikes means out, she finally came to terms with the Met, and made her debut there in 1968 as Carmen. She also sang Eboli, Amneris, and Azucena, but eventually fled from the company because she was miserable.

"When I talk about the Bing regime, it's really unfair for me to say that they were terrible because there were instances when they tried to be very lovely, and at those particular moments I would say the wrong things," the mezzo reports. She cites meetings with the management when they would offer a part—such as Giulietta in *The Tales of Hoffmann,* hardly a star vehicle—and, instead of politely saying she would think about it, Miss Verrett would then and there firmly nix the proposition. "Sometimes I wouldn't even give them the time of day," she continues. "Then it would almost be 'get Shirley Verrett week.'

"And when it was suggested that I sing at a gala they were having, there were people very high up in the administration who felt, 'she's not one of us.' Robert Herman [former assistant manager under Bing] was one of these men. He would try to bend over backwards to be lovely, except I always felt it wasn't truthful and that used to get to me. Those eyes of his, ooh."

Aside from the displeasure over the repertory offered her, Miss Verrett also disliked the way the Bingians did business and ran the company. "I used to sing and *dash,* because I couldn't stand the atmosphere," she recalls. "I treated them very badly with a feeling of joy inside, except that it doesn't make for great relationships with people. I stayed away from the house for the last few years of Bing because I was hoping to come back and be a part of the new regime, whom I really do truly love as people. But if it hadn't worked out with them either, I would have said forget it. I would not go through a lot of trouble again just to say I'm singing at the Metropolitan."

Her strategy worked out beautifully, and then fate stepped in to assist her further. Initially, she was scheduled to sing only Cassandra in *The Trojans.* But when Christa Ludwig, the Dido, fell ill, Miss Verrett replaced her in the opening night performance, becoming the only singer on record to have done both parts in an uncut version of the Berlioz epic. Luckily, she had sung Dido five years earlier in a Rome radio broadcast.

Starting in 1975, the tall and striking mezzo will begin revealing a new side of her art. She hops on Gioacchino Rossini's bandwagon for the first time anywhere—as Neocle in *The Siege*

of Corinth and Rosina in *Il Barbiere di Siviglia,* both at the Met. The American is also planning to give Europeans a sample of her chutzpah when she invades soprano territory as Lady Macbeth at La Scala in 1975, and as Norma at Covent Garden in 1976.

Coinciding with the excitement and fulfillment of professional success bordering on superstardom, Miss Verrett has finally filled a gap in her personal life by becoming a mother. In 1973, she and her husband, a white painter who prefers to remain nameless, adopted a lively and smiling light-skinned daughter, Francesca.

Perhaps life does begin in one's forties. But why has it taken this long to reach the prime of Miss Shirley Verrett? Because the mezzo is a mulish-minded woman whose lifelong conflicts have been resolved by listening to no one but Shirley. These days she's still charting her own fiercely individual course—and watch it if you get in her way—but there is one major difference. "I listen to people now, I didn't before," Miss Verrett admits.

Born in New Orleans, the young Shirley moved to Los Angeles with her family because her father, a building contractor, felt that there would be more opportunities to get work there. On the West Coast she enjoyed a typical middle-class existence which, in the early fifties, led to her becoming both a CPA and real estate broker. She always wanted to sing, but her father, independent in his own business, decided it would be wise to have something to fall back upon if her artistic aspirations didn't work out.

It was during her brief interlude as a businesswoman that Miss Verrett began to study voice seriously. In 1955, when she won first prize on Arthur Godfrey's "Talent Scouts," she came to the attention of Marion Freschl, a voice teacher and Juilliard faculty member, who arranged for her to receive a scholarship and also began teaching the fledgling. While at Juilliard, she won a number of competitions as well as engagements, which earned her professional experience even before she graduated.

Meanwhile, not everything was coming up roses in her personal life. In 1951, despite her mother's warnings that the man she was about to marry was no good for her, stubborn Shirley plunged in anyway. After six months of disappointment she knew Mama was right, but it took her until 1959 to unload the unwanted spouse. Then, four years later, after swearing she'd never wed again, Miss Verrett took the marriage vows once more—this time to a white man and a Catholic to boot.

Luckily, there were no familial objections on the color issue from either side. As for the religion question, by then it had been answered anyway. You cannot be a Seventh Day Adventist in good standing and wear lipstick, bracelets, and rings, let alone get divorced and appear on stage in theatricals. Shirley knew there could be no middle ground: It was either her church or herself. "I had to become aware of what I was as a human being without flying off in ten directions because I was thrown by the strictness of the religion," she recalls. "When I finally decided to go into opera, I said if God has to punish me because of it, then He has to, but I have to do it. I still have a religion, I believe, but it's all in here," Miss Verrett says pointing to her heart. "More than that, I try to be true to myself."

The singer is blessed with a luscious voice which, on first hearing, appears to be a mezzo. But she is also equipped with a freak upper extension which allows her to pound out high notes with the ease and sound of a soprano. While Madame Freschl was completely convinced that her student was a mezzo, the student wasn't nearly as sure. During classes she would sing as a mezzo, but at home she would vocalize as a soprano—another conflict.

Finally there was a showdown, and Shirley announced to her teacher: "Okay, I'll work with you as a mezzo, but wherever my voice leads me, I'm following. And if it means I have to be a coloratura, that's what I'll do." And that's what she has done, which accounts for her peculiarly varied repertory today. Whatever happens in the future—and Miss Verrett hopes it will have a lot to do with Bellini, Donizetti, Rossini, Meyerbeer, and perhaps Wagner, and little to do with Verdi—she categorically refuses to be pigeonholed. In fact, she wishes that programs could simply say Shirley Verrett, Singer.

In the early sixties, while she was forever saying no to the Met, Miss Verrett's plight was made easier by a full schedule of recitals plus the beginnings of a European career. She debuted as Carmen in Spoleto in 1962. The next year she sang the gypsy girl in Moscow and Kiev and then brought her to New York and the City Opera in 1964. La Scala and Covent Garden heard her in 1966, and since then she has become a regular at both houses. And, in 1968, she relented and came to the Met.

Today, although she figures prominently in the Met's plans, she is—as only a prima donna could be—a trifle miffed. "I do get a little bit upset with them because, for example, Covent Garden says to me, whenever you want to sing whatever, if it's within our power, we'll put it on. La Scala is the same way. I want to do *La Favorita* at the Met. I've requested it, and said I wouldn't ask for too many other things if I get it.

"If they do it, there are two people up for the lead role, Marilyn Horne and myself. I think I should be the one to get it. To give it to her would be a mistake, and it's not because she's not a fabulous singer. Look, I believe in credibility on stage. I like Marilyn, we're friends, but she does not look the part of a seductress. It's sort of cruel to say, but if you're going to put certain operas back in the repertory, let everything be as right as possible, let the principal singers look as if they're lovers."

Miss Verrett has other ideas about opera management as well—like getting rid of singers who can't sing anymore, most of whom are leftovers from the Bing regime. As an example, the mezzo cites a well-known vocalist who was assigned a starring part in the new production of *L'Italiana in Algeri* during the 1973–74 season. "When I saw that cast, I said what is *he* doing there? He hasn't been able to sing anything for five years, honest to God! He sings coloratura like . . ." Here Miss Verrett launches into a brutal imitation. "Now that's bad! This is one of the reasons why my husband, Lou, refuses to go to the Met, except on certain occasions. He always says, you will not drag me there, Shirley, I'm sorry."

Her husband is probably the only person Miss Independence will listen to regularly. She credits him fully for building the financial aspects of her career, but most significantly for giving her insights into her own character. "If it hadn't been for Louie, who is white, I would have been one of those blacks who are sort of out of it because I was brought up very well, had enough to eat, a nice home, and was properly educated. I would have almost been white, being black, if you know what I mean. One day Lou told me, you'd better wake up Shirley and start looking around you and seeing what is happening. He said, you don't have to be bitter, just be aware of what is going on so that you don't get to be like a person who is of another race and says, 'but why are *they* demanding things?' "

When she speaks of her husband, it is with obvious deeply felt love. "We're lovers *and* friends. I like Lou. I would like him just as a friend if I weren't married to him. I feel he has made me a better singer because I'm happy. Right after we got married, people used to say, Shirley, the voice is different. I suppose it's because of happiness and contentment and all those corny words which work for me. And now with the baby people are again saying, hey, there's another dimension to the voice."

It should come as no surprise that the individualistic Miss Verrett is not, as opposed to many career women, in conflict about motherhood versus profession. "Sometimes parents feel guilty because they do what they do," she says. "I'm not guilty. I'm a singer, that's my work. Daddy paints and teaches for a living. Live with it, my dear. When you grow up, you do what you like."

That does not include Francesca bragging about her mother, the internationally renowned opera star. "To keep her away from that, I will divorce her from certain activities. But I want Francesca to be with me whenever possible. And I want to be home when she begins school. But there's one thing she has to understand. She lives in a house with a painter and a singer. That's our life, *basta*."

17

A Comer: Kiri Te Kenawa

WHEN KIRI TE KANAWA stepped out for a solo curtain call following her unexpected Met debut in February 1974 as Desdemona, the earshattering uproar that erupted was accompanied by cascading confetti sent down from the balcony by opera freaks who shredded their programs to bits in a spontaneous and supreme gesture of welcome. The fetching New Zealand soprano (pronounce her name Kih-ree Tuh-KON-a-wa) also bowled over the critics who were un-animously enthusiastic about "what may be one of the great voices of our time," "a voice as international as the Met itself," and acting that was "touching and invariably believable."

Miss Te Kanawa had done it before—created the kind of wild sensation that keeps opera and its buffs alive and clapping. It had happened in December 1971, when her performance of the Countess in *Le Nozze di Figaro* at Covent Garden elicited such a fervent response that her triumph was reported inter-nationally. But no one at the Met was prepared for what occurred on February 9 when, on three hours' notice, Miss Te Kanawa jumped in for the indisposed Teresa Stratas in the season's first *Otello,* which happened also to be the nationally broadcast matinee. Luckily, she was not unprepared, since she was sched-uled to make her debut in the same opera a month later which turned out to be her second performance.

The Te Kanawa message obviously got through quickly enough for Schuyler Chapin to be in evidence after each act to personally escort the lady of the day to her dressing room. Caught up in the frenzy of the backstage madness, the general manager happily and breathlessly talked about "a sensational artist, a lovely person." Tenor Jon Vickers, the Otello, wore a smile a mile wide and kept murmuring, "Isn't she wonderful! Isn't she wonderful!" The object of all this adoration, chic in a cream-colored dressing gown, kept her cool admirably. "I feel fine, I feel good," was all Miss Te Kanawa had to say in between graciously accepting accolades and signing autographs.

A few days later, comfortably ensconced in her West End Avenue sublet, the soprano was far more verbal. "I didn't sleep all night after the performance. I stayed up till ten the next morning," she reports in a proper English accent. "It's the first time that *ever* happened. Usually, I crash after two hours. Coming to the Met has been a terrific hurdle to get over. I'm thrilled to be able to make my debut now. I would have been too old soon," she giggles.

Kiri is already enough of a prima donna to know that her age must remain undivulged. "I'd like to say I'm twenty-four," she quips. When this fails to register the correct reaction, she giggles again and compromises. "Okay, let's say I'm under thirty and shall remain under thirty for the next ten years." She'll probably get away with it. Kiri is a kooky charmer, five feet eight and a half inches tall and sturdy, with enormous brown eyes and loosely flowing brunette hair. Her exotic good looks stem from her odd parentage.

The soprano is half Irish and half Maori—and if that isn't glamorous enough, there is more to her genealogy. On her "mum's" side, Kiri is descended from Sir Arthur Sullivan, of Gilbert and Sullivan. On her dad's side, she hails from the great and famous Maori warrior, Te Kanawa. It's no wonder she's been leading a fairy princess sort of existence.

"I'm extremely proud of being a Maori," she says, eager to talk about a favorite subject. "They go back to 1440 A.D., I think. They inhabited New Zealand first, from no one knows where. Some say Peru. The white people have only been in New Zealand for about two hundred years. The Maoris are not becoming extinct, although there are not many pure Maoris around. Quite a lot of white boys marry Maori girls.

"I'm reasonably medium dark-skinned. There are those much paler, with ginger hair and blue eyes. But I'm not a typical Maori because I was brought up by a white mother who was very domineering. Being Catholic, I was taught by nuns in a convent. I thought it wasn't so hot to be a Maori then. The children were cruel to me because I was different—'that Maori girl.' I was the only one in the school, and they picked me to pieces. I was also not a pretty child—dead ugly. I'm still not very beautiful either, and I'm not being silly. If I ever came back in the world, I would *love* to be gorgeous."

As a child, Kiri responded readily to her mother's desire that she become a singer. "I loathed every minute of school because all I wanted to do was sing," she reports. "My mother told me I was going to be an opera singer and that I would go to Covent Garden. When I was fifteen, I was sent to Sister Mary Leo, a singing teacher at St. Mary's College in Auckland, and then I started entering competitions and winning prizes and small bits of money. I like competitive work—that's the white in me. The best thing you can say to me is, 'You can't do it.' Then my Maori pride starts working."

Late in her teens Kiri went to Australia, won the prestigious Melbourne Sun aria competition and was heard by James Robertson, director of the London Opera Center, who invited her to study there. She got a grant from the New Zealand Arts Council, dropped out of school and went off to England. At the opera center, she was soon appearing in lead roles and then, in 1969, she auditioned for Covent Garden, sang the Countess' first aria in *Le Nozze di Figaro* and was offered a contract—to include the role of the Mozart heroine which later catapulted her into prominence. She tried out the role by coming to the United States and singing it earlier in 1971 with the Santa Fe Opera.

Initially, Kiri was a mezzo. But when she began studying in London with her current teacher, Madame Vera Rozha, whom she adores, her voice started going up and up. She believes that it has now grown to the point of being a heavy lyric. Kiri, who calls herself an instinctive singer, will concentrate in this repertory area, performing such roles as Desdemona, the Countess, Mimì,

Marguerite, Donna Elvira, Fiordiligi and, eventually, Violetta, Tatiana and perhaps even Lucia.

At the Met her first season, she did a total of four *Otello* performances. During '74–75, she will sing a run of Donna Elviras, but the season after that, unless something can be worked out, she will not be appearing at the Met at all.

Although she is greatly in demand and booked until 1978, Kiri is determined neither to push her voice nor her career. "I'm trying, in fact, to hold it back as much as I can," she explains. "I keep being reminded of other people who shall remain nameless because they're still singing—but not very well." In this, as well as in most other areas, she is considerably influenced by Desmond Park, an Australian mining engineer whom she married in 1967. He came to New York for one of her performances.

To understand her relationship with Des, as she calls him, is to understand Kiri. "We met on a blind date in London and got married about six weeks later, although we weren't in love at all. I've no idea why we did it, but it turned out to be the best thing in the whole of our lives. Love grew, and it's growing all the time. It's just divine. It's very hard to explain, but when I'm with Des I have his character, which is strong and quiet. He can overpower me at any time. Once he says something, that's it."

Kiri considers herself quite liberated despite the fact that she is literally programmed by her spouse. "I am an instrument with buttons to be pulled and pushed, I really am," she says, smiling. "I love to be organized. Des says that one must always be feminine and controlled. When I first met him, I was wild and would do the stupidest things. Now, although I'm much more controlled, I'm still not allowed to buy anything unless I ask Des. I'm in chains and I love it. I used to spend everything before I earned it just because I was unhappy."

These days she's reasonably happy, but by no means flipped out because of her new-found celebrity status. "My life in many ways is quite a turmoil and difficult to cope with because I get myself so stewed up about things. I get very lonely, but I can't do very much about that, I'm afraid. I am also very vulnerable to affection. If someone says they like me, I'm so thrilled. It's awful really, but I just love to be loved—for me as a person and not as a performer. This is a very big thing, a whole problem with me."

But it's also given Kiri a perspective which allows her to view her career realistically. "When I won the Melbourne *Sun* contest, I thought I was the greatest thing since sliced bread and that everyone was in love with me. But when I went to England, I soon realized that people are very fickle. Now I can assess them at face value very quickly.

"I'm happy, I really am. There's nothing like being down to earth. What the hell can you get from these flowers?" Kiri asks, pointing to the endless bouquets which fill the living room —dying mementos of her Met debut. "It looks like a funeral parlor in here. We're still in New York. We're still on the sixteenth floor in the E apartment. The world is still going around, right?" Right.

18

House Director:
Nathaniel Merrill

ISTORICALLY, THERE HAS BEEN so much cliché-ridden clap-trap passing for stage direction in opera, one has to assume that being an operatic *régisseur* must be one of the most irksome and unmanageable tasks in all of the performing arts. For the director who has overseen more productions at the Metropolitan than anyone currently, there are two particular enigmas central to the difficulty of his job. The prime puzzlement omnipresent in any operatic undertaking, according to Nathaniel Merrill, is "to.be able to stage an opera, create the action, and then turn it around so that it looks like the music was written as an accompaniment. I'm not saying that music should accompany the theater, but in opera the action should look so integrated with the music, one shouldn't be aware of the dividing line between them. In other words, it should look like the music has been composed for that action."

Beyond seeking this Olympian ideal, Merrill would also like to know "how to make somebody into a diva or prima donna, how to give them that special pizzazz that when they walk across the stage everybody watches them. If I had the key to these two tricks," he laughs, "I would be the best director in the world. But nobody else will ever know them either, so it doesn't worry me."

Merrill has come to be something of a specialist by accident at the Metropolitan. Although his first new production—in 1960—was of the comedy *L'Elisir d'Amore,* he soon became known as an able crowd-handler and was therefore assigned operas with the worst traffic problems as well as some of the biggest shows the company has ever mounted, including *Les Troyens, Frau ohne Schatten, Rosenkavalier, Aïda, Meister-singer, Samson et Dalila* and *Turandot.* He has also tackled such "lighter" works as *Hansel and Gretel, Luisa Miller,* and *Parsifal.*

An admitted establishmentarian from whom one can expect little or no gimmickry, Merrill is the kind of director who is never self-serving. Whether he is working on an epic or intimate production, his directorial approach is always on the basis "that opera is fundamentally a musical art, and the theater of opera doesn't exist without the music." His credo is *never* to go against the music, and he is very suspicious of his colleagues who talk about "opera theater." Merrill insists that "opera is basically *not* theater. I really think that if you approach opera principally from the theatrical standpoint, you don't get opera in its best sense."

As a specific example of what he means by placing musical values over theatrical ones, Merrill cites the Italian film version of *Aïda,* released in the fifties, starring Sophia Loren with the voice of Renata Tebaldi. 'I''ll never forget Miss Loren who is a wonderful actress and beautiful certainly," he says. "But the contented smile she used to mime the words had nothing to do with the aural excitement of the music, which Tebaldi would have been able to convey on the screen, although she isn't as good an actress. At least she would know that when the high notes came, this was going to be an exciting moment—and she would have been excited about it. Miss Loren, on the other hand, was placid. She could differentiate between the words, but sometimes when the words are exciting, the music is not always at its high point."

Merrill, the idealistic guardian of music, is totally realistic when it comes to the practicalities of directing at a house such as the Metropolitan. "There is unfortunately not much time for experimental direction," he reports. "Too bad, because it tends to make you a little bit more conservative. The really outlandish ideas are probably discarded before you go into rehearsal if you know what you're doing, because there is very little time." The director is also a popularizer. "I really believe that opera is played for the public," he proclaims. "It is a form of amusement, not funny ha-ha, but entertainment where the biggest trick as a director is to somehow grab hold of the public in the first two minutes of the piece and drag them in."

Merrill's productions speak for themselves and they can never—for better or for worse—be mistaken for the work of such theatrically oriented directors as Sarah Caldwell, Walter Felsenstein, Frank Corsaro or even Franco Zeffirelli. Considering his rather middle-of-the-road attitudes, it is not at all surprising that the Massachusetts-born typical New Englander has achieved such longevity at the Metropolitan, an organization hardly known for its theatrical daring. He joined the company in 1955 as an assistant stage director and within five years had graduated to having his own new productions. Although he works elsewhere, the Met is home base. "It is the greatest opera house in the world," he announces. "Our dramatic standard is very, very high, and we have a large number of rehearsals. I had more rehearsals for *Hansel and Gretel* at the Met than I had for *Otello* in Hamburg."

The director is a great believer in getting down to essentials. Although he often speaks with a touch of smugness and is thoroughly convinced of the quality of his work, he does not play superstar when it's rehearsal time. Once in the theater, he feels a director must be thoroughly organized and that his homework should be behind him. Merrill speaks with disdain of colleagues from the legitimate stage and films who arrive at the opera house without the least idea of what they're going to do. Their laziness, he feels, causes the chorus, in particular, to become undisciplined, while the well-known singers simply lose respect for their dramatic leader. "Most of the solo singers at the Met really do know their own business," he reports. "They also know right away whether a director knows what he's talking about or whether he's mucking around. Too many of my colleagues muck around and it's reflected in the attitude that the singers give them."

Merrill speaks from experience, having worked with about every international biggie except Joan Sutherland. The director truly enjoys singers as people, feels he understands them and thinks he gets on with them splendidly—their peculiar quirks notwithstanding. "Dealing with these big personnel is a question of making them feel secure, making them feel that what you are trying to do is in their best interest, not yours," he explains. "The problem is that when they become superstars, they are usually not young anymore. As established singers, they know exactly what tricks are going to work for them. If you're directing *Falstaff* and have an experienced Sir John, you're going to have a very hard time when he comes with a rose to Alice. He is going to take the flowers out of the vase and put the rose in because he knows it's going to get a laugh, it always has.

"If you can substitute something better which will work, and convince these people and get them to put their trust in you so that they will give up their clichés, then, perhaps, you will have a way to work with them. Look, they've probably done it thirty different ways. One could really stage an opera by saying: You enter like you did in Milan, walk to the table like you did in Rome, and everything else is Visconti from Covent Garden—except don't forget the new bit we've added about picking up the napkin. With some singers you have to come to grips and say, 'Come on, tell me, what are you going to do here?' And there is no point in forcing things. If a tenor can't sing a high C lying on his stomach with his feet in the air, don't make him. He won't ever do it well anyway."

If Merrill has ever lost a battle with a superstar, he can't recall it. He remembers "discussions" with Maria Callas and other hotheaded ladies and gentlemen, but no losses. "Singers want to be told things the same way children want to be disciplined," he says. "They want the security of knowing that they're going to go here and it's going to be all right. I know that Franco Corelli sings every duet standing on the same side of his leading lady. It is his habit. But if you know it in advance, it gives you a strong weapon because you're able to stage the whole opera with him singing all his duets on that side—but without him ever realizing how he got there. When Corelli worked with me, he felt very much at ease because he never had to go to the 'difficult' side or move the soprano over. I never had any trouble with him. In fact, I would rather have him than any other tenor I know in a production. In his heyday, it was the best tenor sound and the best tenor singing."

Merrill is secure enough to pass musical as well as theatrical judgments because he is by training a musician. He studied to be a composer in college and graduate school and also seriously played the clarinet. He gave up the latter because he was no good at it, and the former because he wanted to do more than just sit in a symphony orchestra. He came to directing because it seemed the next most logical choice. He is also married to a musician, the talented Metropolitan assistant conductor Louise Sherman. The couple works together at the Met whenever possible, and most always on outside jobs.

Ever since college, music has been Merrill's major driving force. Curiously, he believes that "people are not pushed around enough by music. I'm pushed around terribly. Sometimes it drives me so that I cannot sleep. I find a strong recurrent beat of rhythm with a melodic line imposed on it irresistible. I think very few people are sensitive to the point that they understand what music is written to portray. Therefore, to get people to relax on a stage in front of other people and submit to this is difficult. I think, however, I have the knack to some degree of stirring people up so that they're willing to listen, forget some of their inhibitions and let the music push them around."

Or let Nat Merrill push them around: He makes no bones about enjoying his position as boss. "Directing is power. There's no question about that. I don't like the misuse of it, but I do like it and the feeling of being able to create." He also takes his work so seriously he can almost always be found at the opera house whenever one of his shows is running. This is most unusual—particularly in contrast to the majority of European directors who leave immediately after opening night, probably never to be seen again until they have a new assignment.

Merrill explains his penchant for overwork. "You see, I have a slightly different position. It's untitled, but being the leading director or whatever at the Met, I have the responsibility of keeping my productions as tight as possible. There's no question that when Rudolf Bing didn't come to the opera house one night, things were slack. Very cleverly, he was usually seen at the beginning of the evening, and no one ever knew if he was there for the remainder or not.

"In the same way, my presence is important. I'm not saying

I'm there as a traffic cop to punish the children because they ran the wrong way. But psychologically, their seeing that I care enough to come when I don't have to makes them care enough to do a little bit extra. It's that extra bit that makes it better, and that's why, if I may say, I think my productions hold up more than those by other directors."

19

Glamour Boy in

His Middle Years:

Thomas Schippers

THOMAS SCHIPPERS IS FORTY-FOUR and grown up. Middle age is no trauma for the former kid maestro because, even at fifteen, he was smart enough to know more than the score. Happily ensconced in Philadelphia's fancy Curtis Institute of Music, little Tommy Wunderkind had the perspicacity to perceive far beyond what the curriculum provided. He recalls those days vividly. "At the end of every week, we had recitals. This one came out, that one came out, and they all played very well. Then a young pianist named Sherman Frank came out. He was the best-looking boy EVER. I sat there in my little balcony seat, and I just couldn't believe it. Sherman played like a God! But nobody else thought so. Sherman was so good-looking that no one ever listened to what he did. I had to think about that a lot."

If Schippers is implying that he was the second best-looking boy EVER, no matter. Cast in a classic Grecian-god mold, the kid from Kalamazoo could then—and still can today—run rings around most of Hollywood's male marvels. But, like poor Sherman, poor Tommy had to put up with a lot of people who looked but didn't listen and a lot of critics who wrote about his haircut instead of his music. So he's a little touchy about the subject, and if you ask him how far he's gotten on his looks alone, Schippers becomes more than a little defensive.

"All that nonsense of you can't be talented and handsome and at the same time do it all when you're young bores me so much, I don't think about it anymore," the conductor sighs. "My only argument to that febrile attitude is: Then why in hell is Schippers still around twenty-five years later? Because, let me tell you, lack of success may be difficult, but it is even more difficult to sustain a successful career."

The maestro is being modest. His career might better be described as explosive. Starting at sixteen, when he was already established as a Metropolitan Opera coach, Schippers embarked on a wild and wonderful giddy-paced existence that has only of late begun to subside a bit. The first orchestra he *ever* conducted was the Philadelphia. That was at eighteen. At twenty-five, he became the second youngest conductor in the history of the Met (Walter Damrosch had him beat by three years). That same year he made his New York Philharmonic debut. In both cases, the associations have been long-standing ones: Schippers is one of the most frequent guest conductors with both organizations. Abroad, he established early on a continuing relationship with La Scala, and has led the Berlin, Vienna, London and Israel Philharmonics, as well as appearing at Bayreuth, Covent Garden, the Rome Opera and the Teatro Colón in Buenos Aires.

Beginning in the mid-fifties and continuing well into the sixties, Schippers was one of the most talked about—for the right and the wrong reasons—of a bumper crop of dazzling young maestri. Few denied that he was genuinely talented, musical and an electric presence on the podium. But there were those who were taken in by a lot of glamorous publicity and extramusical considerations, and thought of him as being grand, aloof, a playboy and a social climber. This faction really licked their chops when the most dashing of all celebrity bachelors married into one of the most prominent of all social families. Then the portrait of the young upstart was at last complete. Only, according to the subject, it was a big fake.

"I *could* have done all those things I was accused of," Schippers exclaims. "I had every right to. I had the world by its tail, but I didn't swing it. I didn't even swing as a matter of fact. Some people think that Schippers is fancy, or that I have a photographic memory because of all the music I have learned. I have conducted, and this is true, 118 operas in my life. I began

when I was twenty. But when you figure it out year for year—
and I didn't do the counting, someone else has—somehow I
had to learn these works. I wasn't leading a secret life. While
everybody thought I was playing, I was really working my balls
off.

"I was always a loner until I got married. Then I was very
much alone in my marriage, rarely having a so-called New
York social life. But, when I did, it would be a Suzy Knicker-
bocker who got hold of it. Those people who thought it was
the kind of life I was leading could assume, in fact, that it was
so because it was being reported on. What can I say? It was
all false. I didn't do it!

"I was also never a trouper in the sense of having Metropolitan Opera singers in my house for dinner. I don't have fun
sitting down with a lot of colleagues. I want to play bridge, talk
about painting. I have a very full life without being intellectual,
please, but those musical soirées, no. On Met tours, I would fly
in for a performance and fly out. I was never around the pool.
I never did any of that, ever—ever—ever."

It's paid off in that, while others have come and gone,
Schippers has remained. He has survived being a child prodigy
and Wunderkind. He has survived an aura of phony glamour
that frequently both clouded and made light of his very serious
musical intentions. He has survived the death of his young and
beautiful wife in 1973. And he has survived recent bouts with
his own health.

It may not have been easy, but professionally Schippers is
none the worse for his efforts. As it has always been, his career
today is international. Aside from regular guest stints with the
world's major orchestras and opera houses, he is music director
of the Cincinnati Symphony, director of special projects for
Italy's radio and television network RAI and co-music director
of the artistically ever burgeoning Spoleto Festival, which he
founded with Gian Carlo Menotti.

As Schippers himself is the first to admit, there were certainly many raised eyebrows when he accepted the Cincinnati
post in 1970. The music world could barely contain itself from
snickering. How long would the sophisticate last slumming in
the provinces, the cynics asked. What they all failed to realize
was that, for his own musical welfare, the job in Cincinnati was

the best thing that ever happened to Schippers. There was even a glamorous aspect to it all—he was named to the post without having ever conducted the orchestra. But what really mattered was that, finally, the peripatetic maestro had a solid American base from which to work. Now he could settle down and show that he was not only willing but able to sustain a serious endeavor, instead of hopscotching all over the place. Not that Schippers feels that he had or has anything to prove; it's just that a lot of other people do, especially those who are still blinded by the razzle-dazzle of the young Tommy Wonderboy.

Schippers adores both the city of Cincinnati and its orchestra, and his feelings are very much reciprocated. Such is the civic pride in the maestro and his men that a building in the downtown section of the city once displayed a sign which said, "Jesus Saves," next to one, displaying a picture of Schippers, which proclaimed, "The Best Musicians in the World Follow This Man." Of course, Schippers sweatshirts are also very much the rage.

"I don't want to make it too much of a Shangri-la, but every rehearsal with them is a happening," the maestro says enthusiastically. "I don't know what the reason is, their heritage or what, but they are certainly, beyond a doubt, the best behaved orchestra in the business, which helps an awful lot because you don't have to fight all that banter. I must say, at least for the moment, that this is where I am the happiest.

"The people in Cincinnati are sophisticated to a point that doesn't make any sense in a so-called Midwestern city. But it's really the beginning of the South, and that must be the reason for the big difference. Also, after San Francisco, I think it is physically the most beautiful city in the country. You get away five, ten minutes from downtown, and it's like the Rhine. We all live on the river, which is fat and beautiful, and there are big hills everywhere. I eat breakfast with twenty-five cardinals every morning, and I live ten minutes from my dressing room in Music Hall. Incredible!"

Schippers is of the old school when it comes to disciplining an orchestra, which is perhaps a music director's most important and difficult task. Luckily, he gets no flak in this touchiest of areas. "Cincinnati is the only organization left in the country where not only is the music director Hitler," he reports, "but everybody wants him to be, *including* the orchestra men. And where music is concerned, I'd say I'm pretty much Hitler."

Schippers is sure he has changed the orchestra, which he announces as being first-class, but finds it difficult to explain how. "If I have made a difference, it comes down to sound, and that's impossible to describe. I have given the orchestra a sound, and I don't think I did it by teaching it to them. There's the chemistry of various components—the sound of the hall, the sound of the stage, the quality of the stage—and what happens between a conductor and an orchestra, which no one has ever been able to explain."

Schippers is a sound freak and, in an effort to illuminate what he means, asks and answers the question: Describe the difference between a Brahms symphony conducted by Toscanini and by Bruno Walter. "The difference is mostly sound. This legend of Toscanini having an incredible ear is only partially true. Toscanini had an incredible musical or technical ear. He was the kind of person who, in a flamboyant squirmish of the piccolo would hear a flute where another conductor might not. But his ear for sound was not good, and I'm here in front of the whole world to say it.

"I knew him well enough, was with him long enough, and heard too many performances and rehearsals to know that he did not have an ear for orchestral instruments or singers. I don't care what the world says, the NBC Symphony was not a first-class orchestra. The music he made with them was incredible, but man for man, it was not the best talent one could find in New York, and the group was created for him. So that kind of ear he did not have. Bruno Walter did. The sound he made in a Brahms symphony was so much more beautiful than Toscanini's, for me there was no comparison."

His preoccupation with sound influences the way Schippers conducts the Cincinnati as well as the ensembles where he is a guest. There is a world of difference between being a music director and concentrating on one orchestra which knows you as intimately as you know it, and being a guest conductor, when the ambience is totally altered and results have to be achieved in a much more compact, less personal manner. It is an art to master both techniques. Many maestros are *either* great music directors *or* great guest conductors. Some, like Schippers, seem to be able to handle both successfully. It is a subject that the conductor has often pondered.

"I was shocked in an emotional way years ago when Herbert von Karajan guest conducted the New York Philharmonic. I made a point of being around, and since I was already a conductor, I could smell what was happening in the rehearsals. First of all there was the drama of how all the Jewish boys were going to take to von Karajan. That was beautifully vanquished after ten minutes. He was very limpid, very casual, very nice, very relaxed. After a half hour, they knew they were dealing with a first-class conductor. What von Karajan did not realize was that he was a guest conductor. He was treating the Philharmonic as though it was the Berlin or Vienna, where he was never a guest, but *the* conductor.

"We make sound. We can't explain how, but in the end perforce it has to be with our bodies. What I could tell in the rehearsal between von Karajan and the Philharmonic was that what he wanted, from the way he was using his body, was not happening in the orchestra at all. And it wasn't because they were being rebellious. It just wasn't working.

"In the *Jupiter,* he was so impressed with the winds he got carried away and overlooked rehearsing the symphony. It was a disaster at the concert, by which time it was too late to do anything about it. He also did a big Strauss, *Zarathustra,* I think. It really didn't come off either.

"I knew, even then, why. It was because of von Karajan. He didn't have his own orchestra, and he had forgotten how to teach. Because when you are a guest conductor you are also automatically a professor. You have to be well enough prepared. You have to know the orchestra that you are conducting. I've gotten to the point now where my programs are geared to the orchestra, *not* to me."

While he is professionally secure and content, personally Schippers is by no means fully adjusted to the loss of his wife, who died of cancer. His endless administrative responsibilities keep him occupied, but not enough to fill the void. He wed the lovely Nonie Phipps in 1965. Theirs was a brief but happy life together. "I'm not feeling sorry for myself," the widower says, "but I'm not over it yet and I know it. We really didn't have a chance. We were married for nine years, and yet I feel we were just getting started.

"I have aged fifty years, but in a good way, I hope. Before Nonie died, I think I always felt that people didn't die. It wasn't that I hadn't been exposed to death before; I just didn't think she was going to go. Fortunately, she knew. The only reason I still keep the apartment here in New York and the house in Cincinnati is because she told me to. Whenever she felt that she was getting to be too much for me, she would go off to Cincinnati, which she adored. The house there is kind of special, and she would try to pick herself up. She told me at the end, 'I was never lonely in that house, and neither will you be.'

"The one place she did not mention was a house I built for her in Corfu, which was paradise, the end of the world, no roads, nothing. That, I have no feeling for anymore. It's strange. Whatever she told me to do, I have done. Sometimes it seems like yesterday, sometimes not like a year ago, but another lifetime. At this point in my life, I'm just trying to stay above."

Alone. "I'm a hermit. I was never a hermit before; I was a loner. Friends have not turned out to be any relief. Work has not. Study has. I'm not a TV man, I haven't eaten in a New York restaurant in ten years. I never go out, so I find myself here at ten o'clock at night. I talk to myself like we all do, and I know it seems wrong, but I'll pull out my Russian grammar book and study instead of calling somebody or doing the normal thing.

"There are two obvious ways of getting over what happened to me. Most people use one's friends, and you escape yourself by being out with others. I'm not built that way. Nonie ordered me to forget her as quickly as possible. It helps. That's why it sometimes feels that it was not a year ago, but twenty years ago. Other people have given up houses because they reminded them of the person. If Nonie hadn't ordered me not to, I would have.

"I cannot live this way all the time, but at the moment I must. I tried living with someone for three weeks last summer, and it was disaster. It wasn't fair to her or to me. It wasn't even hell, but black, negative. I don't mean to sound like a bore, but I relax studying Russian. I'm doing it to prepare for the new *Boris Godunov* I'm conducting at the Met. I get a kick out of the complications of the *grammatica*. Having gone through Greek, everything else is easier, but still not that easy."

Schippers has been told that he speaks Greek, Italian and French flawlessly and without an accent—which is pretty funny when you consider how he sounds speaking his native tongue. The maestro is not unaware of his peculiarly grand accent, and has winced mightily when hearing it coming back to him on radio or television. "I hate it," he admits. "It is not an affectation, but it's there and I know it doesn't work. It's pretty bad. I don't even know where it came from. Of course, Americans who don't know very much say that I have an English accent, which is completely wrong. Certainly if I'm in London, I do not have an English accent. But when I hear myself on interviews, for example, which I won't go on anymore, I really sound like the fun they used to make of Stokowski. I must say his accent never improved with age."

Perhaps his mania for getting to the heart of a language through an in-depth study of its grammar is an outgrowth of the singular manner in which Schippers probes a musical score before conducting it. Recently, he had his first fling at teaching and, suddenly being forced to verbalize what he had been doing unconsciously for years, enabled him to understand more thoroughly his own modus operandi.

"I never realized how much you can learn about music and about yourself until I taught at the Conservatory in Cincinnati and had students plying me all the time," Schippers says. "These so-called doctoral conductors were so terrified of the so-called masterworks that I soon understood—which I never would have done without them—that no matter how young you are, no matter where you are, if you're conducting a Beethoven symphony and are shy about it, you'll never get through it. You must have the courage of your own musicianship to be able to sit down with Mr. Beethoven and discuss his problems as well as your own.

"There isn't a perfect work in the world, and every composer had his difficulties. If you're not a musician enough to realize where Beethoven in any particular symphony had his problems —whether with form, orchestration, melodically or rhythmically —you can never feel that you have the complete right to conduct that piece. I tried to convince the students that they must not be so timid in front of a Beethoven work."

Of late, Schippers feels that he had not always been able to practice what he preaches. "I complain to my secretary, to everybody, that what I have lost in the last two years—because of Nonie—is a lot of time. I want to get back to my real passion—studying. I would rather be a monk in my cell than I would stand on a podium. I don't think that performers give themselves enough time to study. It is a secret, lonely passion and it can only be done by yourself.

"If you're conducting four times a week, forty-eight weeks a year, tell me how are you going to find the time? Just recently a friend asked me if, because of Nonie's death, I had lost interest in my career. I said, on the contrary, what you don't realize is that I was doing in my twenties what most conductors do in their forties. So try to realize that a lot of beautiful dirty work has been done already, let's say, on *Carmen*. I remember how I learned *Carmen* over a period of three years. I really took it luxuriously. I would study for five hours in the morning, go to half a movie, come home and study another five hours. This would go on for weeks. But I still didn't conduct it. I let it go. The next year I did the same thing, and so on.

"It isn't that I don't have the time to study that way now. Thank God, after a certain point, studying becomes quicker as you grow older, but I still know it is the only way I can get into a work. It's like a game. Take *Manon Lescaut*. I pretend that I'm not Thomas Schippers and that I'm not reading Giacomo Puccini's masterwork as far as I'm concerned, but that we are doing it together. In fact, when I study a work, I begin from the composer's point of view. No matter how good or bad the libretto is, I do realize that whatever came out of his pen was inspired by the words. Opera begins there. So when I learn a new opera, I'm not a musician at all. I must start out as a stage director.

"Everyone said that my *Manon Lescaut* in Spoleto was different. In all modesty, I think I myself know that it was different. All conductors hope they are conducting the best performance of a work, maybe the best performance ever. I think when you try too hard to do that, you're usually making a mistake.

But if you have the courage, and I know it sounds old-fashioned, of sustaining a colloquy with the composer, you can't go wrong."

There's something else too. While Schippers is not exactly insecure about his own podium abilities, he is also not above learning from others—to the point of imitating them and admitting it. His grasp of diverse repertories is extraordinarily wide and, although he admits to feeling most at home with Schumann and Donizetti (in themselves an odd couple), he appears equally at ease with Anton Bruckner and Samuel Barber. Much of his facility for handling differing musical styles comes, no doubt, from listening very closely to masters of a particular genre.

"I have never been afraid of imitating," he exclaims. "I remember when I first thought about *La Traviata*. I could sense the naïve and open beauty of the Prelude, but I really didn't know what to do with the pitter-patter, for lack of a better word. Then I heard the old man [Arturo Toscanini] in Italy. I thought there was something wrong with my ears. In the Prelude, he came to the pitter-patter, and he played it as if every note was the beginning of the fifth Beethoven. When I conduct *Traviata* today, I do it that way, too. Call it copying if you want; I think imitating is a better word. Maybe if I really thought about it, I could pin down where I got each musical style from. I surely know where my feeling for a lot of last century's music comes from."

Schippers is referring to a remarkable grande dame called Victoria McGlaughlin, who taught him piano from six to twelve while she aged from ninety to ninety-six. It is perhaps idle to speculate on the effect an early teacher had on a very young lad, but there is little doubt that without Miss McLaughlin, the musician we know as Thomas Schippers would be a very different kettle of notes. It would be going too far to say that the son of an electrical appliance dealer would not have turned to music at all, because little Tommy was already at the piano at four. But it was Miss McLaughlin, above all others, who gave him the art in all its glory and without any static.

"Working with Victoria was exactly like all the cheap, fictional music biographies of the last century," Schippers recalls with amusement. "It was literally with the ruler, with the top of the piano coming down, and with me having broken fingers for four days. She could still play herself, and when I wasn't doing well would sit down and show off. It was unbelievable how she could still carry on. Of course, the pedal was down all the time, which taught me how they played one hundred years ago.

"It was fantastic for me because she was living at the time when I would have wanted to live. I was going out of my mind with all the stories, but even though she would tell me about the first performance of *Tristan* and how she was with Brahms when he was writing the Third Symphony, I studied nothing but Bach, Beethoven and Mozart. Victoria was born in Vienna, and don't ask me how she got to Kalamazoo, Michigan. Anyway when I was six, seven, eight, whatever, my first excursion— indiscretion—was to go to the music store on my own and find a G. Schirmer edition of the piano versions of all of Wagner's operas. I started playing them, and I didn't sleep at night I felt so guilty being carried away with Wagner. Of course, I couldn't dare tell Victoria about it. My next infidelity was Debussy. I knew she'd throw the whole piano at me for that.

"I really had to sneak anything but the three classic masters. I remember even then knowing that I was going to have the most beautiful life possible. If one month there was a Wagner and the next month a Debussy, there had to be more. And there always was. Like most children, my family fought against my being a musician. They didn't fight my going off to Curtis, because that was a nice, big fat scholarship. But I was certainly going to come back after Curtis and go into business. There was never any doubt in *my* mind, however. I always knew that I had no choice. There were other things I could do, but nothing else I wanted to do. I still feel that way."

And so the young genius went off to Philadelphia and the Curtis Institute in 1945, aged fifteen. Within a year, he was earning a living as a church organist and choir director. He studied the piano, tinkered with the fiddle, but his passion was composing. "Had anybody asked me at sixteen what I was, I would have said a composer," Schippers recalls, of his youthful mania which came to naught. All his musical activities notwithstanding, the budding creator went off to Yale to study philosophy. A year later he was back in Philadelphia. By being patient, he finally got to Olga Samaroff, with whom he studied piano. "For a year and a half I did nothing else. Eight hours a day at the piano, eight hours a day composing. I was very happy. Then Samaroff died, and boom. I swear it was just because I was frantic that I entered the conducting contest of the Philadelphia Orchestra.

"I did it to relax. I didn't know what I was at that point, so I thought well, I've tried everything else—even the oboe. But I didn't enter the contest to win, but just because it would give me something definite to prepare for. The repertory demanded was everything, and I had never conducted before, other than waving my arms in church. For nearly a year, I prepared the repertory, desperately looking for help. There was no one with time, so I did it on my own. Somehow I ended up as one of the finalists. And that meant an interview with Mr. Ormandy."

The celebrated maestro was most understanding about how the brazen kid had lied by three years to get into the contest which was open to ages twenty-one and over. "He gave me a small Hungarian laugh when I told him," Schippers recalls. Talent will win out, and sure enough, Tommy Schippers ended up conducting the Philadelphia Orchestra, the first ensemble he had ever led. The program consisted of the Mozart *Jupiter* and Beethoven Second symphonies and the complete Stravinsky *Petrouchka*. It is the last he remembers best. "I was so scared. I'll never forget walking out and seeing all those French horns. All their bells seemed to be turned to me. I tell you it was like facing a battlefield. But I did it. Ormandy likes to say I won, but it really isn't true. I came in second."

While this seems the perfect occasion for Schippers to have begun his conducting career, curiously he did not pursue the craft then. He considers the incident "an accident." He was still intent upon being a composer, and to support this fancy was still busily involved in a number of churches. To understand the next "accident," one must remember what he was up to during the period between sixteen and eighteen, when he entered the Philadelphia Orchestra contest.

Although he was studying at Curtis, Schippers was also spending a great deal of time commuting between the City of Brotherly Love and New York, where he coached a young singer named Anne Riley. Thanks to old Victoria's training and those private indiscretions at the Kalamazoo music store, teen-ager Tommy had no trouble sitting at the piano playing and coaching anything or anybody.

Miss Riley also employed another coach, Karl Kritz, who was

an assistant conductor at the Met. One day, much to her delight, the vocalist was invited by Kritz to attend a *Tales of Hoffmann* rehearsal which he was preparing for a senior colleague at a West Side studio. Much to everyone's distress, the rehearsal pianist didn't show up, and Kritz wasn't able to locate a replacement. Anne suggested Schippers who, luckily, was in town that day.

He recalls the incident with relish. "I had never seen *Tales of Hoffmann* before in my life. But I was born to sight-read. I can't teach it, because I don't know how to do it, but I *can* read anything. Well, I was *such* a hero. All the singers—even Karl— were kissing me." Karl did more than show affection. He got on the phone quick to Max Rudolf, then an assistant manager at the Met, and as Schippers says, "told him there was this freak in town.

"A while later, Max called and invited me to his Riverside Drive apartment. He was irresistible, self-contained but with charm. He asked me if it was really true that I had never seen *Tales of Hoffmann* before. I told him yes, and that I didn't even know who wrote it. Then he really got down to business. On the piano was the orchestral score to *Salome*. I read nine or ten pages and, one week later, I was a coach at the Met."

Because of his Met activities, by the time he was nineteen, Schippers was well known enough among singers to be in demand as a private coach. He even opened his own studio, where many of the Met's biggest names, including Eleanor Steber, came to work with him. Schippers today believes that, "I've always understood singers. It sounds very prosaic, but I really do. I know five bars ahead, for example, if they're going to slip. How I know, I don't know, but the fact that I do makes them, I think, sing better." The singers, being proud and fond of their unusual find, always recommended him when a crack keyboard man was needed at the last moment. Thus, he got to the Lemonade Opera, where he "conducted" two-piano performances of such forgettable works as Mendelssohn's *The Stranger* and Prokofiev's *The Duenna*.

And then in technicolored storybook fashion, the day came when one of his students—whose name Schippers can't remember but should—phoned and asked him to play at an audition. The young coach had a deal with his charges that auditions were out because of time. But there were extenuating circumstances and Schippers relented. Off he went to the Morosco Theatre where, in the most primitive conditions, he *stood* and played a truncated piano *offstage*, while his student sang his heart out onstage. "As we left the theater," Schippers recalls, "this cute girl asked me for my name and telephone number. I shall never forget the next day. I was packing to leave for a South American tour with Eileen Farrell when the phone rang and somebody said, 'This is Gian Carlo Menotti. Was it you who played yesterday at the Morosco Theatre?' Then and there he told me he was writing a new opera called *The Consul,* and would I be willing to prepare the singers for the Broadway production? I must hand it to Gian Carlo. He had the ears then. He knew nothing about me other than the accompaniment he heard on a lousy piano."

Schippers, of course, accepted the post and added to his duties by playing the piano in the pit. *The Consul* opened in Philadelphia, and then came the day when—you guessed it—the conductor got sick. "Chandler Cowles, the producer, called me in the afternoon and said, 'Tommy, you are conducting tonight. I am bringing over the score right now.' I couldn't speak. Then Gian Carlo called, and I knew there was no choice. Believe me, there was none of that, aaah, this is my big chance. I figured that the orchestra would help me, because I wasn't ready at all. In fact, I got terribly sick and developed such hemorrhoids that I could not walk. I shall never forget Chandler and the stage manager putting me on a chair and carrying me from the Ritz-Carlton Hotel across the street into the pit of the Shubert Theater, where I started conducting *The Consul.* Very badly, I would judge. Believe me, I don't know why anybody fell for me at that time."

The musician is neither indulging in trivial chitchat nor fishing for compliments. He sincerely believes that, prior to 1955, "inside I didn't know what I was doing." And he sticks to his guns despite the fact that Pierre Monteux, Charles Munch and Victor de Sabata all apparently disagreed with him. This holy trinity, it seems, appeared one night at a *Consul* performance in Paris, a few months after the Philadelphia incident, and were so impressed by the fledgling conductor, spread the good word throughout the continent and, in essence, laid the foundation for Schippers's European career.

Back in the States, the young talent, in his early twenties, joined the staff of the equally green New York City Opera. The years there were not all happy ones. "I did kitchen work," Schippers exclaims. "The glamorous kid swept the stage, pulled the curtain and did everything but conduct. Nor was I anxious to conduct. I wanted to learn about opera, and indeed I did learn. Then, finally, I guess it was Laszlo Halasz who asked me to conduct *Hansel and Gretel*."

Present in the audience the night of Schippers's debut were his old friend Max Rudolf and Rudolf Bing. Soon, the young maestro was summoned by Bing, who offered him the chance to conduct three repertory operas at the Metropolitan. "I can't deny that I was excited and didn't know what was going on," Schippers says of his first meeting with the general manager, "but I apparently had a built-in perception of what had to be done in the preparation of music. So I started asking questions about casts and rehearsals. The singers were fine, but the rehearsals were a shock—a reading with the orchestra, a stage rehearsal and that was it.

"I'm sure I stumbled around for a few minutes and then said, 'Mr. Bing, I can't come to the Met and do *Carmen* with two rehearsals.' He said, 'But you have conducted *Carmen* before, haven't you?' 'Yes,' I said, 'but that's beside the point. I could have conducted *Carmen* one hundred times, but I still need to work on it.' 'That's all we have on our schedule,' Bing said, and there was a freezing silence.

"Unfortunately, then I said, 'But Mr. Bing, I don't understand. I know Dimitri Mitropoulos and I know what his rehearsal schedule is here, and he conducts repertory operas, too.' Then, as only he could, Bing said, 'But Mr. Schippers I needn't tell you that Mr. Mitropoulos is an internationally famous, very important man.' I said, 'That's why I need the rehearsals, Mr. Bing.'

"That was it. We all walked out. I still have the letter Bing sent, telling me something to the effect of, 'I consider you a very stupid young man and as long as I am general manager of the Met, relations between us are severed.' Well, I was finished. It was terrible."

The next reel of *Portrait of an Artist as a Young Bigmouth* runs like a fifth-rate Hollywood movie starring Troy Donahue as Tommy Wonder. But Schippers "swears" that it is all true, and relates it with the breathless fervor of a prayer-meeting participant.

"A year and a half later, I was still at the City Opera, and I couldn't stand it any more. We were *so* bad. I was there at ten in the morning, and if I was home by one in the morning, I was lucky. It was a penal colony and our performances were, I must say, terrible. By this time Joseph Rosenstock was in charge. I was making $60 a week, which I needed, but I didn't care. I was going to give up my job. I felt dirty, and I was frantic.

"One day I called Rosenstock's office and insisted that I see him *that* morning. As I walked out of my apartment building, I received a cable from de Sabata inviting me for my first concerts at La Scala. I read it in the subway, and I don't know if it gave me encouragement or not. When I got to the City Opera, the switchboard told me there was a call from my manager, Bruno Zirato. I told them to tell him I'd call him back in an hour.

"I went down to Rosenstock's office and I couldn't have been firmer. I told him I was leaving, that I cannot make music this way. His plum to get me to stay was a new production of *Don Pasquale* that coming spring season. I said thank you, it's too late, no matter what you offer me I cannot stay here any longer. It took me an hour to convince him and I walked out sweating.

"I called Bruno and he said, 'Tommy, I don't know what is going on, but Mr. Bing wants to see you immediately.' Within an hour I was seeing Bing. He was full of charm, and guess what he wanted me to do. A new *Don Pasquale*! He said, 'Mr. Schippers, you were so concerned the last time about the singers the Met would offer you, would you be kind enough to go over to that corner and write down the four singers you would like for *Don Pasquale*. The charm of that encounter was that the four names I wrote down were exactly the same ones they wanted to give me.

"My God! There we were! You can imagine I was going crazy. How can the City Opera offer me *Don Pasquale* at 11:30 and the Met offer me it at 12:30? I was frantic. I went home and I swear to you there was a call from California because I had been, speaking of good looks, forced into a contract with MGM when I was eighteen. They, once again, were offering to make a film with me. I thought the whole world was going crazy. At this point, I flew out of my apartment and, just to escape, went to the nearest theater and walked in without even looking at the marquee. Guess what I walked into? Don't tell me it was not a fateful day! *100 Men and a Girl*! I sat through this horror of Deanna Durbin and Leopold Stokowski, and that finished my movie career. That made it very easy for me to go home, call my agent and say, forget it. I never ever made a film. It was quite a day. And it's all true—true—true." Whew.

All that happened to Schippers in the following years—including such plums as being in the pit on the opening night of the Met's new home in Lincoln Center—is almost anticlimactic. Perhaps the least exciting on the surface, his Cincinnati appointment, will, in the long run, prove to be far more significant than the razzle-dazzle of his early years. And, of course, with a personality as electric as Schippers's, there are still always some goodies forthcoming. In the 1974–75 season, he will conduct two of the Metropolitan's five new productions—*Boris Godunov* and *The Siege of Corinth,* which will bring Beverly Sills to the opera company.

Whatever he does now or in the future, there is little doubt that, as a musician and a person, Schippers is a changed man. The boy they used to call Dorian Gray is in his Middle Period, a widower much saddened by tragedy, but hardly bitter, still effusive, still exuberant and still endlessly energetic. He doesn't look forty-four, nor does he act it in the sense that he can be rather agreeably boyish. But there is nothing youthful about his attitudes when it comes to something that is important to him—be it bridge, painting or, of course, music. Then he is the venerable maestro, spouting pronunciamentos like gospel. Perhaps it is because of the stability of Cincinnati, or that he has enough offers to fill the calendars of two men, or more significantly because he has absolutely nothing to prove anymore —whatever, he is thoroughly convincing in his musical sincerity, theatrical exaggerations notwithstanding.

"I can honestly say I haven't lived without a sheet of music for one entire day of my life," he muses. "I think that's rather shameful. But I will also say that standing in front of an orchestra is not the greatest thrill of my life, either. There are quite a number of conductors around the world who must feel that it is, or they wouldn't conduct as much as they do. Maybe being the boss of these 106 men is what is important to them. But all their activity cannot come from the hunger to make music, because you cannot make that much music in one year.

"As I said before, if you're conducting four times a week, forty-eight weeks a year, how are you going to find the time to study? I cannot get out of me what I cannot get into me. That is a vital definition of conducting. My emotional theory is absolutely this: If you are a first-class conductor and you conduct something you know and believe in, it will, without fail, work."

20

The Guild:

Dario Soria

I'S CURIOUS THAT AS THE EPIC financial crisis at the Metropolitan continues along a disaster course, the financial assistance it receives from the Opera Guild continues to increase. In this most critical of periods, it must be comforting for the company to know that the Guild remains tried and true and puts its money where its mouth is to prove it: In 1974, it handed over more than $3 million to the Metropolitan.

The Guild's ability to keep the money rolling in stems primarily from the manner in which it is run today—strictly as a business, with none of the former overtones of social club, plaything for wealthy, idle patrons or part-time do-gooder group. The prime force behind the inauguration and sustaining of this practical and contemporary outlook is the organization's new managing director, Dario Soria.

An Italian Jew who fled from his homeland in 1939 and emigrated to this country, Soria, sixty-two, has a history of association with successful and classy products (Angel Records, the Soria Series on RCA). Much of his class has rubbed off on the Guild. But this is a bonus; Soria's operation is founded on solid, realistic business techniques and dedicated to the proposition that volunteers and professionals must work hand in hand.

This is good business, too. After all, it was—and to a lesser degree still is—the volunteers who were responsible for the Guild's success in the first place. Back in the fall of 1935, the Met was in a depressing situation frighteningly reminiscent of the current one. General Manager Herbert Witherspoon had died suddenly the spring before, a few weeks after taking office. His replacement, Edward Johnson, a charmer if there ever was one, had plenty of singing experience but absolutely no history in management. Add all of this to a ghastly post-Depression financial mess, and it spelled doom for the company.

In the midst of the turmoil, a tireless visionary named Mrs. August Belmont came up with a plan: "Thrashing around for ways and means to maintain opera, the thought occurred to me that it might be helpful to form a union of opera-minded men and women, charge them modest dues—say $10, $30 and $100—and offer tempting advantages in exchange, such as ticket service to performances or attendance at a dress rehearsal.

"Large posters on the front of the opera house and a few advertisements in the papers were almost the only concessions the management of those days made to 'selling' opera. What if an organized group of volunteers should take the cause of opera to the public, introduce the artists at public luncheons and receptions and adopt regular campaign procedures? It followed that I should call the union a Metropolitan Opera Guild."

Thus, Eleanor Belmont's brainchild was born. Like its creator, who went on to become something of a legend and surely opera's grandest nonsinging grande dame, the Guild too evolved over the years into what is now a flourishing operation.

Although legally and by structure totally independent of the Met, the nonprofit organization is so closely allied to the house that it might as well be part of it. Its objectives are really quite simple: "To support the Met and bring audiences into it," Dario Soria says, seated in shirt sleeves in his bright and uncluttered office on the top floor of the Bible Society Building, a few blocks south of Lincoln Center.

The Guild goes about this deceptively easy-sounding task in myriad ways. In essence, however, the entire operation rests heavily upon one cog in the wheel—the group's greatest calling card and foremost publication, its magazine *Opera News*. Such is the incredible potential of *Opera News,* Soria bluntly links it inseparably to the Guild's future growing ability.

Why the magazine is so central to the operation is simple to understand. By a quirk of fate, it is the only publication in this country devoted to opera. As if this weren't enough of a wallop, *Opera News* is also unique because of the role it plays in communicating with the Met's national audience, those countless, faceless souls who tune in on Saturdays to hear performances live from the stage of the house over the Texaco-Metropolitan Radio Network.

During the twenty-one weeks when the matinees are broadcast, *Opera News* serves as a program guide, devoting an issue in words and pictures to every conceivable sort of information about the opera of the day, including background stories, musical analyses, interviews, timings of the acts and popular intermission features. When there are no broadcasts, *Opera News* then becomes merely a magazine reflecting its name.

So, the Guild has a good thing going here, and it knows it. *Opera News* is available only by subscription. (Some 650 copies per issue are to be gotten at New York City newsstands, but try to find them.) And the only way to get the subscription is by becoming a member of the Guild. There are many ways of accomplishing this, because memberships are on different levels: Sponsor, $200; Donor, $100; Contributing, $60; Sustaining, $35; Educational, $25; and National, $15. The more money one spends, the more goodies one gets in terms of rehearsal passes, luncheons, parties, etc. The cheapest way to get one's hands on the magazine, then, is to plunk down $15.

By now it should be very clear why Soria puts so much weight on *Opera News*. The magazine provides a splendid inducement for drawing in Guild members. At the close of 1974, the Guild had 70,000 members whose dues reached an all-time high figure of $1,500,000.

That may sound impressive, but in reality it is not impressive enough. "Why do we only have 70,000 members when the broadcast audience alone must be, conservatively speaking, 1½ million?" Soria asks. "We obviously haven't done what we should. We've always tried to reach the 100,000 mark and we will continue to try."

Since Soria's arrival at the Guild in 1971, the organization has switched advertising agencies and is currently involved in systematically reviewing, modifying or changing every piece of Guild advertising and promotion material in an effort to boost membership.

Of course, the Guild offers its members more than just a subscription to *Opera News*. In the publications area, it prints an annual engagement calendar plus a number of special supplements like the 1973 Caruso 100th anniversary issue and a first stab at a snazzy Metropolitan Opera Souvenir Booklet.

Its Ticket Service, in existence from the early days, has taken on a sophisticated approach, including a telephone order system available to members after office hours. In 1974, subscription and single-ticket sales amounted to $1,768,000, and more than 16 percent of the total Met box-office sales in New York.

Like its luncheons, lecture-teas, rehearsal passes and backstage tours, the Guild has always been involved in benefits. These generally take place on the night of the first performance of a new production or at a special gala. Festive and dressy occasions, they give members a rare chance to be where the action is—and to pay for the privilege while at the same time supporting the Met. In 1974, there were five such occasions, and they netted $445,000, or $250,000 more than the $195,000 cost of the house.

It is in the field of education that the Guild feels it is least contemporary, and is therefore currently involved in reevaluating all of its services from student performances to teaching guides. "When the student performances began," Soria explains, "New York was a smaller city, and there was certainly a smaller community interested or even conceivably having access to opera. Since then, both New York and its population and the whole field of education have changed radically.

"Today, we can approach education in two ways. First, the selfish one, that our motivation is to build audiences of the future for the Met. Second, if there is in the community a group of young people who would be interested in opera, but might miss it completely, not having the chance to actually be exposed, do we bypass them altogether or should we try to give them the opportunity?

"Because of the limitations of the house in space and time, we have to go to the schools. But what do we bring? Do a piano and one singer really have any resemblance to the real thing? Goeran Gentele believed that either you bring something into the schools which is opera, whether in chamber form or otherwise, or you are misleading the children and giving them a first experience that may turn them off forever.

"We're making an experiment in the spring of 1974. We've commissioned a one-act opera from Al Carmines, with a libretto based on the story of the duel between Alexander Hamilton and Aaron Burr. It will be a chamber work with eight instruments and eight singers, and will be performed in costume with props by members of the Met Studio in school auditoriums around the New York area. One of our board members, Patrick Smith, made a gift of the commission.

"We also will certainly continue student performances in the house plus the Look-ins, which started in 1973, with Danny Kaye continuing as host. The problem here is that everything gets out of proportion and the costs become enormous. What we're going to do is stop giving one group of children a three-act opera. Bear in mind that most of these kids have never been to the Met before. The impact of just coming into the house itself and seeing the chandeliers rise is already an experience.

"With a double bill like *Cavalleria Rusticana* and *Pagliacci,* we can get two groups of children in, one for each opera, for the same cost. The same with the Look-ins. Instead of each visit being 1½ hours, it should be fifty minutes, tight. This way we have two audiences for the price of one."

In 1973, the Guild introduced 7,500 kids to the wonderland of opera via the Look-ins. Such was the popularity of the Gentele-conceived program that 14,000 youngsters had to be turned away. In all, besides two Look-ins and thirty-four varied student performances in the house and at schools, plus passes to rehearsals and reduced-price tickets for regular performances, Soria estimates that more than 90,000 young people were exposed to opera in one form or another.

Just as the Guild is desperately trying to keep abreast of contemporary trends in education, so is the total organization coming into the twentieth century with a bang. Unfortunately, much concerned with opera, and the Metropolitan in particular, has had a mustiness about it. There are people who still consider the Met—and the Guild—a rich man's club, a social entity. This may have been true once, but it isn't today. And yet, even a man as knowledgeable as Soria at first fell for the stereotype.

"I must admit," he says smiling, "that initially I thought this was not a full-time job, and that it involved committees and ladies and so forth. But I found out very soon that this was not the case. As for the social aspect, whatever the Guild was in the past, it never had a closed membership. All you had to do to get in was to pay your dues. I think that the social restrictive thing that may have been associated with the Guild really isn't there today. The way people get on our board is not on a social basis at all.

"Look, I'm a foreigner by birth, I'm certainly not society and I'm a Jew. If the Guild was what you would have associated it with in the past, I couldn't possibly function happily here. I think things have been dusted off."

Although Soria is delighted by the progress the Guild has made under his brief aegis, and talks incessantly about the wonderful heads of departments, staff members and cooperative board, he is not fooling himself about certain undeniable circumstances. "Just to restrain my euphoria and self-congratulatory tendencies, let's face it, it must not have been easy to do business with Rudolf Bing. I realize that one of the reasons a number of things happened that coincided with my taking over had to do also with the fact that there was no Bing anymore.

"Inflation, of course, also makes our figures bigger because the dollar is worth less. In terms of real dollars, the figures are still impressive, but not as big as all that. We feel this, because no matter what we give the Met, it doesn't go far enough."

Soria wants to give the Met more, but does not believe that the Guild should broaden itself much beyond the current setup. He feels that more money can be squeezed out of the publications area, with more special booklets, a Guild book club, and maybe, very cautiously, records. "But it's all really linked to *Opera News* and membership," he says with finality. "We'll have to find ways to bring more people in."

21

Opera News:

Robert Jacobson

N KEEPING WITH HIS DETERMINATION to realize fully the enormous potential of *Opera News,* Dario Soria has brought in a new editor, Robert Jacobson, to run the magazine. The move was less of a slap in the face to Frank Merkling, the former chief of sixteen years who retired in the spring of 1974, and more of a decided attempt to rejuvenate and perk up a very conservative publication.

Just how conservative was brought to light with a resounding ouch by a 1973 survey which unearthed the shocking fact that the mean reading age of *Opera News* is fifty-two. Much to his horror, Jacobson was greeted with this news upon joining the staff, and although it was always understood that the thirty-four-year-old editor would give the magazine a youthful accent, he immediately had to own up to a rough job ahead of him, strictly in terms of developing a new readership.

"Even though the Guild and *Opera News* are growing by numbers, we are not growing with young people," Jacobson explains. "To build for the future, we're going to have to find ways of reaching kids in college or just out. They're obviously going to opera. In places like Boston, Houston and Seattle, the big appeal of the companies has been to youth, not just to the old-fogy audience."

Jacobson is part of a Guild committee working on a plan to

give college students a chance to get *Opera News* at a reduced rate. Past history has shown that once readers subscribed to the magazine, they renewed. The problem, of course, is how to get them interested initially.

While Jacobson is convinced that the special-price deal might work, he has met with resistance from stodgier members of the Guild. "They say it's not good economics," he reports. "But that's shortsighted. Our current subscribers are going to keep growing older and dying off. If there's not another upsurge coming up underneath, then the whole thing is doomed. It's false economics to be thinking of making money now. This is insurance."

Outspoken and admittedly opinionated, the tall, well-dressed, mustachioed and bushy-haired Jacobson comes to *Opera News* with a long and varied background in music and writing. He studied the former at the University of Wisconsin (he is a native of Racine) and Columbia, and practiced the latter as managing editor of the Lincoln Center Programs for seven years, as well as free-lance interviewer, critic and feature writer for a number of major publications.

His interest in opera is long-standing, and, in fact, was stimulated by *Opera News*. "As a kid, I used to listen to the broadcasts all the time. I didn't subscribe for a while because $10 was something big then. But, from about fifteen on, I began reading the magazine regularly. I still have all the issues in the attic of my parents' house."

Jacobson is eager, optimistic and bulging with ideas, but sober enough to realize that, at least initially, he will have to temper his youthful energies. The Metropolitan Opera Guild is no place for a smart-ass upstart. "There are a number of great people who work for the Guild and do a lot of good," he says, "but they tend to be middle-aged to older ladies who are a little dilettantish. Over the years, there have been pressures brought to bear, and the magazine has reflected them. I think, however, that we're getting out from under that, and beginning to operate more independently.

"There are also a few live wires coming into the Guild who recognize that something has to be done. But it's been a struggle. I don't blame Frank Merkling. Having been here so many years, he was under the influence of the rabble-rousers who said, let's stir up interest for opera and the Metropolitan. It was a kind of crusader thing, which was very good and it served its purpose, but I think that the time has come now to open up the magazine a little more."

Since its inception in 1936, first as the Bulletin of the Guild and then later as *Opera News* magazine, the publication has understandably been considered a house organ of the Metropolitan. As such, there were strict limitations imposed on it, particularly in the area of editorial freedom.

Jacobson cites the major problem—reviews of the Met's and other performances in the popular Reports section of the magazine. "During the Bing regime," he says, "there was for a long time a great censorship of *Opera News* because artists who were on the roster very often put pressure on the management if there was a bad review. Even people like Nilsson and Sutherland complained. They felt that the magazine was an arm of the Met, and if they were written up in it, it should be in a favorable light. This negated anything to do with fair criticism.

"Now, this has ended completely. It stemmed from Bing. Since I've been here, the only kind of editing I've done is to writers who are vicious. That kind of criticism doesn't have a place here, and I'm not from that school anyway. We're not at all censored now as far as opinions go."

Outside of the Met. When it comes to reviews of performances at home, even Jacobson admits there are difficulties. "There is still the old guard that feels the Met should not be criticized in its own magazine, and reviews have been handled with kid gloves. For a long time, performances at the Met were not reviewed at all. It became too complicated and ineffective. But recently, for example, there was one review of a major soprano which was censored. Because she is who she is, the final version was much more delicate than the original, which was harsh.

"I feel, perhaps in blind optimism, that I am another personality to contend with, representing a new turnover which will have more leeway. I believe that I can be thoroughly honest 90 percent of the time. So far, we've had some harsh criticism of a lot of singers. The screaming has subsided. Slowly but surely, we're changing. We're serving the house and we're serving the Guild, but editorially we're not so much a house organ anymore."

Jacobson foresees his own editorial column, which will be

expanded from the current one, as being a forum for his opinions, harsh or otherwise. He even envisions criticizing the Met, but only after the fact.

The major reason for the new permissiveness, according to the editor, is the new general manager. "Schuyler Chapin is a much more modern person than Rudolf Bing. He's enormously co-operative and very much behind us. He views us as an opera magazine." Ideally, this is how Jacobson views the magazine, too—as a publication about opera with its roots at the Metropolitan.

As such, he lists some of the changes and innovations he hopes to make. "One of the things *Opera News* has lacked is timeliness," he says. "It's been occupied too much with background and history and obscure things from the past as opposed to what's going on in opera now. I think we have to become more news-oriented.

"For instance, when an opera is premiered, a four- or five-paragraph report on it by a local critic is hardly enough. It should be covered in depth, with a discussion of what's involved in the creation of a work and how it is put on stage. I don't want to turn *Opera News* into *Time* magazine, but I think the *Time* style of mixing reviews and reportage with quotes is something I'd like to try here."

All of this emphasis on the present is not to say that Jacobson intends to ignore the past. On the contrary, "I believe there are a lot of people coming to opera who are terribly unaware of the past. I don't want to sound pessimistic, but I think that in some ways a great vocal tradition is dying out.

"I'd like readers of this magazine to be aware of what that tradition is. There is so much available via records. I'd like to make this a standard feature, taking it singer by singer and talking about what they stood for and what their art represented. I like ongoing series because they build momentum. But these pieces should not just be silly stories about singers of the past. I don't want them to be musty. All those Mary Garden stories over and over again get very boring."

Although he is aware that *Opera News* has come under fire for not doing deeper musical studies, Jacobson believes that he will have to find the proper balance between musicology and popular analyses.

He also feels that while *Opera News* should cover houses other than the Met in great depth, he is tired of the annual "salute" issues to Chicago, San Francisco and the New York City Opera. He wants to wait a few years before doing a house, and only then writing about it when there is something exciting to tell. He will also extend coverage to include other, less well-known companies, as well as devoting an issue a year to American singers.

As for the companies outside the United States, he envisions a series on great cities of opera, which will in no way conflict with a group of stories the magazine did about ten years ago on the great opera houses of the world.

With an eye toward money, the editor believes that the wealth of material *Opera News* amasses can easily be put to good use in by-products that the Guild could publish. He hopes, for example, to collate an *Opera News* guide to Wagner's Ring cycle. In 1974, the Guild initiated a book service as a test case. About fifteen books, from standard works to recent ones, were offered. If it works out, it will become a regular club-type operation with the Guild having a fine chance to make a nice profit.

From May through November, *Opera News* is a monthly magazine; from December through April, it is a weekly. Jacobson feels that this peculiar scheduling hurts long-term planning and plays havoc with a limited staff during the period they are weekly. He is, therefore, proposing that the magazine appear every two weeks the year round.

Because issues are fatter these days, this regularity would help him produce with much more flow and steadiness. Jacobson expects that the big issues are here to stay because advertising is booming. In 1973, the magazine switched to four-color ads and with the help of C. J. Luten, its aggressive advertising director, sold pages like crazy. Revenue was $188,000, an increase of 35 percent over 1972, and 94 percent over 1971.

Graphically, too, the magazine has perked up considerably, and Jacobson wants even more because he believes that in the past the magazine has occasionally been too wordy and not visual enough.

Finally, because of its increased income, the editor feels that more money should be spent on paying writers. "Traditionally," he reports, "we have been paying eight cents a word. One has to increase that. The best people deserve more. After all, a magazine is only as good as its writers."

It's all very exciting, and Jacobson reflects the enthusiasm in the way he happily speaks about future projects. "I want to make the reader aware that opera is a lively art going on in all corners of the world," he says. "We have to become newsier and livelier ourselves, and yet retain the best from the past. The world of opera is also changing. *Opera News* is still terribly star-oriented, for example. A certain mentality only wants to feature big stars and interview them because it's glamorous.

"But you take places like Boston, Houston and Seattle. There's a new turn in opera there. We should make people aware that it's happening and is going to happen in more and more places. *Opera News* has a tremendous wedge. We're the only ballgame. If we pick up new trends and write about them intelligently and interestingly, I'm sure we can have tremendous influence."

22

An Institution Within the Institution: Francis Robinson

I N THE UPPER ECHELONS of the Metropolitan's managerial staff, there is only one person who spans both the Edward Johnson and Rudolf Bing regimes. That man has been with the company for more than a quarter of a century, and his jobs have been varied. Upon first arriving at the opera house in 1948, he became tour director, a responsibility he still holds. Then, for twelve years, he was head of box office and subscriptions. In 1952, he was made an assistant manager, and since 1954 he has been chief of the press department.

Despite the divergent nature of these duties, the veteran's essential concern has been with public relations. As such, he has been dealing constantly with the Met's image. Coincidentally, his own image has emerged, and it would not be overstating the fact to say that he is a celebrity. In fact, Francis Robinson is something of an institution.

A Southerner with the kind of facile charm that is uniquely geographical, Robinson, sixty-four, is a perfect gentleman. When called upon to play host, he is a quieter male equivalent of Perle Mesta. His distinguished looks, his shiny bald pate, his clothes—always a dark suit, white shirt and darkish tie—his bearing, his style, reek of Old World courtliness. Couple this with a dedicated passion for musical figures of the past, plus a startling ability to reel off all sorts of information about them, and one gets a walking, breathing and very smoothly functioning anachronism.

Perhaps because he must deal with the harsh realities of newspapers, and their often less than gentlemanly reporters, Robinson, suave good manners notwithstanding, can be tough, cool, belligerent and evasive. That, of course, is part of his job. One doesn't last at an organization for more than twenty-five years unless one is an organization man.

The darker side of the assistant manager is seen infrequently, but on those rare occasions one gets the distinct impression that he is not someone to tangle with. Put more bluntly, the Robinson chill can give one terminal frostbite.

To turn the tables and interview the press chief is no easy task. While willing and gracious, he tends to be overly cautious. His blue eyes can take on a devilish glint, and then one knows that a goody is forthcoming, but it is *always* off the record. Robinson is an ingenerate conservative. Rather than providing commentaries on current matters, he prefers reminiscing. He does this at the drop of a hat, on social as well as professional occasions, and does it very well.

"You know," Robinson says, leaning back comfortably in the chair behind his desk at the Met, "Edward Johnson was never meant to be general manager except by God. It's not how well he did it, it's just that he did it at all. He had no preparation. When his singing days were at an end, he talked about coming into the Met administration. His title was supposed to be assistant general manager and he was to have kissed the old ladies' hands and raised money—which he would have been wonderful at.

"Then Witherspoon died in 1935, and they had to get somebody. Johnson took over in the great old British tradition [he was Canadian]. It's just incredible that he could grasp it all. Seven or eight of his fifteen seasons were in the black. Of course, that wasn't all his fault. There was the backwash of the Depression, and the supply of singers from Europe was cut off when the war started. There were also few new productions because of no money. You couldn't get material and labor if there was.

"He saw all that, and discharged it with grace and verve. He was a real leader. There wasn't one of us who wouldn't have gone out and died for him. I'll never forget once when we were on tour and were leaving Bloomington, Indiana, at eight in the morning. It was pouring rain. The singers were stretched out in the cars trying to complete their night's sleep. Spirits were low. But Johnson went through the train singing, 'Oh, What a Beautiful Mornin',' and it was like water on a dying plant. He's never gotten credit for being as good and great as he was.

"Then, along came Rudolf Bing who was extraordinary. He quadrupled the subscription list and nearly doubled the season in New York, as well as giving many great shows."

Robinson is about to dismiss the Bing years with this brief summary, but when prodded continues. "Bing hated people," he says. "If he'd have stepped down earlier, it would have been better. It's very difficult to know when to go. In 1957, when his contract was renewed, he had editorials in both the *Times* and *Tribune*. His stock began to drop in August 1961, with his insistence on closing down the house. He never really recovered from that. You can't tell the President of the United States [Kennedy had tried to assist in the labor problems via Secretary of Labor Arthur Goldberg] he is wasting his time, which is essentially what Bing said."

That rare outburst of honesty over with, Robinson continues his chronology of Met general managers. "It's just too bad that we'll never know how great Goeran Gentele might have been. The *Carmen* indicates something. In fact, the three things he projected, *Carmen,* the Look-ins and the Mini-Met, were all smashing successes. I don't think that's just being sentimental. He again had a way of winning people, and making you want to march to the brave music.

"It's still too early to assess the new regime. But for Schuyler Chapin to strike that unpopular a pose—to tell people that their paychecks will be slimmer by five weeks in the '75–76 season —takes a great deal. He always says that he wants the cards on the table, face up. That's awfully different from what we had two managements ago."

While appearing to favor the current management, Robinson is not happy over a request made of him by the general manager.

The Met's press department supplies—free—a pair of tickets to critics covering performances for publications around the country. Certain outlets, such as the New York metropolitan papers, including the Italian-language daily *Il Progresso,* automatically receive two seats for *every* performance. As part of the drastic cutbacks of 1973, Chapin asked Robinson to save $50,000 a year on press seats. To accomplish this, the press chief had to cut the first-night list (initial performance of every opera) by eleven pairs and every other night by six pairs, as well as halting the automatic tickets sent to the newspapers.

"I didn't like it at all," Robinson reports. "But I also saw how terrible the situation was getting and that Chapin deserved my full allegiance. There have been attempts to cut the list down before, but I warded those off. This time I couldn't, but it's not because I'm battle-weary."

The assistant general manager's staff in the press office includes Anne Gordon, who has been at the house longer than her boss, and David Reuben, a more recent addition. Robinson describes their joint function simply. "To inform the public through the press. Also, to put as good a light not only on a good situation, but certainly on a bad one, and in some cases to try to keep certain things out of the press."

How is this accomplished? "Sometimes by throwing yourself at the mercy of an editor," Robinson says. "For example, the *Times* knew long before we announced it that the new production of *Don Giovanni* was being canceled. But they didn't do anything about it. That was minor; it's happened on bigger stories. What I owe to some writers and editors I could never express."

Before a member of the press will do "favors" for a public relations man, that man has to prove his own trustworthiness. Robinson has a long and varied history of being a journalist and dealing with them, and has obviously mastered this aspect of his trade.

Although he was born in Kentucky, the young Francis moved to Tennessee with his family when he was seven. By the time he was fourteen, the eager lad was working after school and on vacations setting type by hand for the Mount Pleasant *Record.* After receiving undergraduate and graduate degrees (in German and philosophy) from Vanderbilt University, Robinson began writing reviews for the Nashville *Banner,* became a staff member and within two years was made Sunday editor.

Oddly, writing was not foremost on his agenda of things to be done. Opera was in his blood at a very early age. "I remember when I was twelve," Robinson recalls, "that when my father would let me spend the day with him at the phosphate mining plant where he worked, I would take a strip of adding machine paper, put it in the typewriter and make up my opera casts out of the Victor catalogue: *Aïda* with Caruso and Gadski, *Bohème* with Caruso and Farrar. Later, I even studied singing very seriously for a couple of years, but stopped when I knew I wasn't going to become Lawrence Tibbett."

Since there were no music courses given at Vanderbilt and Robinson was hungry for the company of people interested in the art, he majored in German for no other reason than the head of the department was also a leading critic and founder of the Nashville Symphony. "I wanted to talk music with him, so I took every course in German that Vanderbilt offered, even the dialects," Robinson admits with a smile.

In 1938, the late William Fields, who managed Cornelia Otis Skinner, and was the well-known press representative of the newly organized Playwrights' Company, met the active young man in Nashville and was impressed enough with his abilities to invite him to come to New York to assist him. He did, and within no time was involved with such luminaries as Miss Skinner, the Lunts, Walter Huston and Paul Muni. He also got his first taste of touring, initially as Miss Skinner's company manager, and then booking the first transcontinental tour of Alexander Woollcott.

Robinson was beside himself with his new work. It wasn't opera, but theater was a fine second choice, and he had finally made it to New York. "If you had asked me at twenty-five what job I wanted most," Robinson recalls, "I would have said to be Katharine Cornell's press agent. I had it before I was thirty. It was the top job in that field of the theater at that time." At the close of the post-Broadway tour of *No Time for Comedy,* for which he was company manager, Robinson was invited by Miss Cornell to come into her and Guthrie McClintic's office. He remained their press man for five years.

That was during the falls and winters. In the springs, Robinson finally got a whiff of opera, being employed by S. Hurok as a legman for the Met's annual tours, which the impresario booked at that time. Not to leave out a season, in the summers he did publicity for the Boston Symphony's Berkshire Festival at Tanglewood. "I never worked harder and I was never happier," he remembers.

In 1948, Robinson hit the pinnacle, joining the Met as tour director. Currently, he holds the same post, and although the tours have changed drastically from when he first began, Robinson believes they are nonetheless of paramount importance today. "When we go to Atlanta, it's like Mardi Gras in New Orleans," he says excitedly. "It's a great festival time. I can endure a year for that one week. Atlanta may be special, but the same is true everywhere.

"Today touring is not easy on the company, but it never was. Hotels and services aren't as good. Of course, the principal singers come and go as they please, and most of them don't really like it. But a few are smart enough to know, like Lily Pons did, that you have to go to your market. You have to let 'em see you, and know that you're alive.

"We're the national opera company. No other company tours like we do—not La Scala, not Covent Garden—or has the radio broadcasts. Don't forget, the 1973–74 season is the Met's eighty-ninth year and our eighty-seventh tour. Some years we toured twice, and we missed a few during the Depression and war times. But from the very first season, the company went as far as Chicago. We were in San Francisco the night of the earthquake and fire.

"I believe that today the tour public is much more intelligent than it was. *Fidelio*, for example, now does better than it did with Bruno Walter and Kirsten Flagstad. *Rosenkavalier* with Lotte Lehmann didn't sell out in the beginning. Public taste has really improved. Of course, the tour is now six weeks when there was a time when it was ten weeks, and we now go to seven cities when we used to go to seventeen cities."

Robinson's job as tour director includes everything from laying out routes to writing contracts. Whereas he once booked the company into places they had never been before, now he works hard to hold onto the seven cities—Boston, Minneapolis, Dallas,

Memphis, Atlanta, Cleveland and Detroit—they've got. As he says, there are few cities left which can afford the Met or house it properly.

The assistant manager does an enormous amount of advance work throughout the season—lecturing committees which sponsor the tour and generally spreading the good word. "No two cities operate alike," he reports. "Do you know that in Minneapolis they come from Canada and as far as 1,000 miles away to see and hear us?"

Because he has operated on a truly national level for so long, Francis Robinson has gotten to know nearly everybody associated in a major way with the arts in this country. "There are at least two hundred people who, when they arrive in New York, pick up the phone and call me, first thing," he says. "There's no limit to my energy or willingness, but time gets to be a problem."

Add to this the fact that his popular Biographies in Music have been broadcast nationally for more than twelve years on the Met's intermissions, that he had a radio show of his own for two years in New York, that he has been doing special shows for WQXR since 1967, and that he is the author of the book *Caruso: His Life in Pictures,* as well as more than one hundred liner notes for RCA Records, and one understands why the sun rarely sets on the Robinson endeavors.

A quiet evening at home is anything but the norm, yet he is determined somehow to organize things better, particularly his library. "It would be wonderful if, after I go, there'd be a room somewhere with all that stuff. It's unique. Let me assure you, there's no private library like it. Don't forget the files, clips and correspondence alone, not to mention the books and records. Do you know that through all my work, I've never had to leave my living room except a couple of times. That's very comforting on a rainy Sunday afternoon."

Robinson, who will be sixty-five on April 28, 1975, doesn't think about retiring. He jokes, however, that although the Met doesn't have a compulsory retirement age, "they'll probably invoke one just to get rid of me."

The operaphile seems genuinely content with what he's done with his life, and if he's not, he's too active to think much about it. One wonders, though, with his wonderfully resonant voice and suave social manners, whether there is not underneath the well-bred exterior a frustrated performer. After all, he did take those voice lessons as a lad in Tennessee. If he had a wish, what might he ask for? "I should think to be up there singing," he answers with no hesitation. "Not conducting or even writing the music. My God, if it's glorious to hear it, what must it be to do it!"

23

Out Where the Bravos

and Boos Begin.

The Fans

No ONE PAYS much attention to the battered green Volkswagen pulling up to the stage door of the Metropolitan Opera until one of the company's leading ladies emerges from it swathed glamorously in white mink. Then the celebrity-freaks oooh and aaah. Word of the soprano's entrance spreads rapidly through the house. Did you see the ratty jalopy Miss White Mink arrived in? asks one young man of another. The medium Xeroxes this message which eventually reaches a young woman who is crestfallen to receive it. She is the owner and driver of the Volks, a vehicle voluntarily placed at the disposal of the diva. She realizes that a move must be made to halt the badmouthing of the prima donna and to secure her chauffeuring rights. So she purchases a new car.

The concerned young woman is neither in the singer's employ nor a service supplied by the Met to its darlings. She is a fan.

A peculiar breed of idol worshiper nurtured exclusively around the major opera houses of the world, the voice fan is easily identified. At the Met, he or she may be found standing at the rear of the orchestra or in the family circle. The seated fan may be distinguished from his neighbor by the intensity and generosity of his applause and/or by the deafening roar he employs to broadcast a heady bravo and/or boo. Fans may also be recognized anxiously awaiting a dressing room or stage door to open. They're the ones with stars in their eyes.

During a period when the Golden Voices are singing, fans can best be reached care of the opera house. After all, if you're for Corelli, you're probably for someone else as well. Not, heaven forbid, another tenor, but a soprano or a baritone. So if Franco isn't singing, maybe Birgit or Bev or Joan or Sherrill is. Or, maybe it's a debut and you want to check out Albania's alleged gift to the bel canto school. Or, maybe it's some rambunctious mezzo stomping her way into soprano territory. Whatever, you're a vocal astronomer. Unlike your more scientific colleagues, however, your stargazing is done from as close as possible.

A real fan's heart begins to throb when the performance ends. Then it's backstage time when honey flows from tongue to ear, when autograph 3,895 (of the same singer) is added to the collection. If the dressing rooms are out of reach, there's always the sidewalk and the stage door—some way for even the tiniest piece of stardust to rub off.

"A fan is someone who thinks he is the only one who truly understands an artist and if only that artist would invite him up for tea, he'd prove it," says John Coveney, director of artist relations for Angel Records. Of course, die-hard fans have gone beyond the tea stage.

A Corelli zealot has seen the tenor's apartment by helping to decorate it. Nilsson cooks Swedish specialties for her special fans. Caballé courts fans and treats them like kin. Milanov uses fans as escorts. Scotto travels with a fan when her husband is unable to join her. Simionato used to find her refrigerator stocked with prosciutto and melon from Manganaro's, New York's most famous Italian grocery, via a fan.

Artists are hard put to ignore their fans. In the case of the more adoring sycophants, it's a physical impossibility. It's not just a question of New York fans keeping tabs on singers when they are at the Met. A fan who's a fan body and soul will follow his star. It should come as no surprise then that a Corelli enthusiast readily admits to having heard her Franco in New Orleans,

Toronto, Boston, Cleveland, Detroit, Philadelphia, Atlanta, Los Angeles and Mexico City—not to mention Vienna, Paris and Venice.

These devotees are not to be confused with the claque. Where fans stop and the claque starts is when money changes hands. Many observers feel that fans are a subtle form of claquery. But, says one furious fan, "We are not and never have been paid admirers. People don't understand this. Maybe that's why the term fan has developed such a negative connotation at the Met."

Negative is putting it mildly. A former assistant manager of the Met has openly admitted that the Lincoln Center house was specifically designed so that the standees would be as far from the stage as possible. This is a major fan complaint. At the old house, the standing room areas followed the horseshoe. If you were all the way down front, you could wave to a singer during curtain calls and you'd be seen. At the new Met, the fans feel this personal element has been removed and done so spitefully.

Most of Europe's major opera houses treat fans with even less hospitality. Here, fans can get backstage. There, a no-admittance backstage policy is strictly enforced. James Heffernan, the Met's house manager, subscribes to the European policy. "In Paris, I identified myself, was given an orchestra seat but even I couldn't get backstage. It's really unnecessary. It's gotten to be a fad. Who visits you at your employment?"

Fans are able to gain access to the dressing rooms by having their names put on a list which the artists submit before each performance. A fan may write or personally request an artist to put him on the list. Some artists automatically add certain fans to their list. In any case, nothing is simpler than getting backstage. If it's Nilsson you really want to see, but don't know, all you have to do is write or walk up to the new or lesser-known bass in the cast, tell him how much you admire his artistry, and that you would love to see him after his next performance. You're guaranteed an entrance this way. Once you're backstage, who's to stop you from playing musical dressingrooms?

Many observers claim that artists are fearful not to fulfill requests to be put on the list. The singers believe that it is bad public relations. John Coveney reports that certain artists have told him that they put up with the backstage circus for the sake

of half a dozen genuine fans. Coveney says that to the more educated artists, the "hawkers and honkers" don't mean a thing.

Full-time fans are well known to both the star artists and the
Met management. The reigning fan queen of the Met is a middle-aged switchboard operator named Lois Kirschenbaum. Everybody knows Lois. Her appearance in your dressing room means
that you've made it. Her absence is bad news. But Lois is atypi-
cal. She is a star in her own right.

Once, the Met management got wind of a rumor that there
would be a ruckus taking place during the *Werther* broadcast.
It seemed that the Nicolai Gedda fans, furious that their man
was not singing the title role, were going to vocalize their displeasure—particularly when Franco Corelli was singing. Although
this kind of threat is fairly commonplace, a demonstration during a broadcast could prove embarrassing. To make sure their
information was correct, the Met phoned Lois who reported that
a disturbance was indeed planned. Given the word, the Met
ordered extra security guards and everything turned out all
right.

Lois is hardly the heroine of the story, but no other Met
fan can claim to be a one-woman central operatic news agency.
Lois usually knows an entire season's schedule before many high-
ranking Met officials. Lois knows everything and everybody, but
she is more than a fan. She is an institution.

To obtain a more accurate picture of the whole, a survey of
a number of more ordinary fans was taken. What follows are
interviews with three who are different enough, yet representative, to present a fan's-eye view of fandom.

Alice Vrbsky was once backstage when someone asked if she
were a member of the company. A dancer who knew her answered, "No, she just worships talent." This describes the bespectacled geology technician aptly. All the dancer left out is
that Miss Vrbsky does not believe in worshiping from afar.

"I get to know artists first because I admire them," she says.
"People need to have somebody who is interested in them for
the proper reasons. They need somebody they can trust. Apparently they do listen to me because they ask my opinion on
things."

"They" include (in alphabetical order) Raina Kabaivanska, Anna Moffo, Birgit Nilsson and Gabriella Tucci. Just as Miss Vrbsky likes, she dislikes. The mere mention of the name Corelli changes her usual smile to a scowl. "Corelli gets away with a lot," she says. "He has a great instrument, but that isn't enough. He's so unmusical."

Such is the fan's wrath against the tenor, she refuses to buy any of his recordings, even though a favorite soprano may be on it, too. "I just won't pay him royalties," she asserts.

Miss Vrbsky's opinions are based on her study of the vocal art. She herself once played the piano, clarinet and guitar. Always an admirer of the human voice, initially she preferred to hear it in jazz. Her first fan's fling was with Billie Holiday. During the last two years of the blues singer's life, Miss Vrbsky was her traveling companion and secretary.

It was the *Aïda* film starring Sophia Loren and the voice of Tebaldi which attracted Miss Vrbsky to opera. "As of 1959, I really started going seriously—about fifty performances a year, which is my average. At first I was a big Tebaldi fan, but then she stopped singing the way I liked her, and it became too painful for me to hear.

"What attracts me is the beauty of the voice and the feeling with which a singer sings. Whether they communicate. I feel I have to be moved at a performance. It's a combination of a musical and a vocal performance. And, of course, musicianship; I don't appreciate poor musicianship."

Miss Vrbsky usually stands at the Met. Her closest friend among her stable of singers, Miss Kabaivanska, tries to leave her a guest standing-room pass (each artist is given one or two of these which allows guests to stand at the rear of the grand tier level) or a punched ticket (given to artists when a performance does not sell out). Miss Vrbsky is a great believer in applauding her favorites, but will only bravo if she is truly moved. "Wild fans are bad for artists," she says. "I wouldn't applaud as much if one of the people I like didn't do well."

Miss Vrbsky is not a booer. But she admits that she did boo a certain conductor once ("because he destroyed an *Aïda*"), and she always boos the ballet in *Faust*. Perhaps her own shyness stops her from being more vocally negative because one gets the impression that Miss Vrbsky would like to hear more artists told they are performing poorly.

"The trouble today at the Met is that artists know they're not, for the most part, going to be booed," she says. "Today, too many artists are products of publicity. And the American public goes to opera like it was TV. Here I am, they say, entertain me. They don't understand that they have to put something into it themselves."

Miss Vrbsky used to be a charter member of The Line, which at the old Met started forming as early as 5 A.M. ("before the buses were running") to purchase the limited number (175) of standing-room tickets. "Nowadays you don't have to get up too early," she says. "The earliest I've been up is 8. People are losing interest. I myself go to fewer performances."

Miss Vrbsky does more than get up at the crack of dawn for her favorites. To hear Miss Moffo, she has traveled to Philadelphia, Baltimore, Cleveland, Detroit, Toronto, San Antonio, San Francisco, Hartford, Pittsburgh, Chicago and Miami. At the last city, Miss Vrbsky had the odd distinction of being the only member of the Moffo party to arrive on time. She took the bus; the others were on a plane, delayed because of inclement weather.

Miss Vrbsky finances these excursions herself, affording the various ticket and travel expenses "by scrimping along in other directions. I don't buy as many clothes. I also borrow on my pension plan—I might as well live now while I can enjoy it."

How does she manage to travel so widely and still hold her job in the geology department of a New York City college? "Well, for one thing, I've gone to work having only three or four hours of sleep. On local trips, I don't stay overnight. I also take vacation days."

It's all worth the effort for Miss Vrbsky, who feels that "if I see something great, I'll carry it with me for the rest of my life."

"I go to as many performances as possible," says Leon Barry, a forty-five-year-old Brooklyn office worker. "I go not only for my love of music, but for an escape. When I'm at a performance, the world outside is completely nonexistent. I'm elevated. After a really great performance, I have this feeling for days. It's like a high."

A soft-spoken man of even temper, Barry considers himself a fan of music rather than of singers. He does have his favorites, though, and they include Dorothy Kirsten, Licia Albanese, Nicolai Gedda and Beverly Sills. "But I can't say I know many of the artists personally," he says. "I like to keep them on an upper plane. I'm not interested in their foibles. I don't want to confide in them or have them confide in me. Many fans go backstage and are enthusiastic even if the singers weren't any good. I can't do that."

Barry is a confirmed standee. "I stand because I prefer to. If I get too comfortable, I tend to get drowsy. It's a question of finances, too. I go roughly three times a week—sometimes four or five." (Standing room costs $2.85 for the orchestra and $1.75 for the family circle.)

A twenty-nine-year standee veteran, Barry has uncovered one way of saving money. He is aware that Met singers are entitled to distribute guest standing-room passes, and, although Barry is not particularly a Corelli enthusiast, he has gotten into the house on these passes, compliments of Loretta Corelli, wife of the tenor.

Does Barry feel that this is a form of claquery? "Artists give passes to fans because they want them to applaud," he says. "On the times I use a Corelli pass, I applaud because I feel I am obligated to. I like Corelli even though I don't think he's the artist he should be . . ."

But Barry endorses applause. "Fans can awaken audience apathy into enthusiasm," he says. "On the whole, fans are good for artists and good for opera. Especially opera with subscription audiences. Nine-tenths of them go because it's the thing to do. If it weren't for fans, opera would die out."

Positively oriented towards singers, Barry claims to have booed only once—at the first performance of the Met's *Carmen* production. "I booed the choreographer, scenic designer and director. I never boo a singer; I have empathy for them; I know how it would feel." Yet Barry understands how emotions flare up at the opera. "Fans' lives, I would think, are so drab and bare. They have nothing emotionally and maybe nothing even sexually. It's an emotional thing to go to the opera, particularly for fans who have no life to speak of. . . . Fans are basically losers."

Barry characterizes himself as a frustrated opera singer. "Maybe that's why I'm such an opera fan. It compensates for my not doing it myself. Here I am, forty-five years old, yet in the back of my mind, I still have dreams of becoming an opera star. Opera seems to be my whole life, really."

If Alison Ames, an attractive twenty-nine-year-old blonde, gains no other distinction, she will surely go down in operatic history as the gal who invented the slogan, "Beverly Sills Is a Good High," and had it printed on a button. Alison sold the button and turned the profits over to the City Opera.

A rare breed of fan, Alison best describes herself when she announces with mock seriousness: "I have a strong conviction that Beverly could get through a performance even if she knew I wasn't there."

Alison first conversed with her idol many years ago at Korvettes, where Sills was autographing records. "I was completely ignorant of the backstage syndrome and the people who live there. I knew you could go backstage at Tanglewood because I had done so once. So I asked Beverly for a pass to see her there. She looked at me strangely and asked, 'Why only Tanglewood?' And she gave me a blank pass allowing me to see her anywhere. This was folly on her part and she probably wouldn't do it today."

Alison chatters nonstop about her favorite subject. "Anyway, I started going backstage more and more and bringing photos I had taken of her. As I got to know her better, I brought fewer and fewer justifications for my presence backstage."

Alison purchases her own tickets. "I frown on being given tickets. Ugh. I would never say, would you get me in? Beverly has too much on her mind to be bothered with such requests." After the performance, Alison is always among the throng to see the prima donna. "I do the whole backstage bit because I get a buzz out of it. It's fun to see Beverly shaking hands and laughing, and when she sees me it's a whole different expression. That's very nice."

Does Alison talk about a performance she thinks wasn't up to par? "I was really disappointed in the Philharmonic Hall recital one year. Beverly called me a few days after it, and just as I was about to say something, she asked me how I thought it went, and that she felt it went well. What could I say? So I watered down my feelings."

Although Alison and her soprano chat regularly on the phone, the fan has only been to her home once. "She called me and asked me to babysit for her daughter, Muffy. It's not that big a deal that I haven't been invited there more. It's nice to be *intime* with a star, but, for God's sake, leave the poor lady alone. Occasionally, I think it would be nice to go there, but I wouldn't go seeking it."

There are others Alison likes, too, but it is only with Sills that the liking becomes a full-time thing. "I'm not interested in a great quest to meet famous people," Alison says smiling. "It's nice to know them. Every now and then its hits me with Beverly that I know this lady. But I'm not interested in a career of getting to know opera singers personally."

Alice Vrbsky, the serious operaphile disdainful of the unmusical singer; Leon Barry, the frustrated tenor lost in the dream of becoming a star himself; Alison Ames, the Now Generation button-seller doing her thing for Beverly Sills. All fans, all vividly different, all in constant attendance at the opera house, each for his own reasons.

In common they have opera, the sole art form which attracts this kind of obsession and sycophantism. It is perhaps *only* opera —itself painted in such broad strokes—that can encompass such offstage theatrics.

Could even the most rampant rock enthusiast hold a candle—in day-to-day, year-to-year consistency—to the religious, all-consuming devotion of Alice Vrbsky, Leon Barry or Alison Ames?

Index

Index